# THE HOME OF BEAUTIFUL PICTURES

## The Story of the Playhouse Cinema, Beverley

by Peter H. Robinson

HUTTON PRESS
1985

Phototypeset in 10 on 11 point Garamond
and Printed by
The Walkergate Press Limited
Lewis House, Springfield Way, Anlaby, Hull HU10 6RX

ISBN 0 907033 27 X

The Home of Beautiful Pictures is dedicated to my late friend, Aubrey, who gave me years of valuable support for so many of my ideas to bring back and keep films at the Playhouse.

# CONTENTS

*page*

Acknowledgements     ...    ...    ...    ...    ...    ...    ...     5

Foreword by Robert Curry    ...    ...    ...    ...    ...    ...     7

Introduction     ...    ...    ...    ...    ...    ...    ...     9

Chapter 1: Moving Pictures come to Beverley    ...    ...    ...     13

Chapter 2: The Arrival of Sound     ...    ...    ...    ...    ...     28

Chapter 3: The Sound of Sirens     ...    ...    ...    ...    ...     38

Chapter 4: A Time for Change and Innovation    ...    ...    ...     42

Chapter 5: Eyes Down    ...    ...    ...    ...    ...    ...    ...     53

Chapter 6: A New Light ...    ...    ...    ...    ...    ...    ...     66

Chapter 7: The End?     ...    ...    ...    ...    ...    ...     81

Chapter 8: A New Beginning    ...    ...    ...    ...    ...     83

List of Ernest Symmons' Films     ...    ...    ...    ...    ...     87

# WHY DID I WRITE THIS BOOK

Over my many years of involvement with the Playhouse, I felt it was about time I committed to paper many of the stories I have had passed on to me by Mrs. Symmons and other cinema staff. The 'bits' I had heard often spurred me into wanting to find out more, but I never got around to it.

In early January, 1984, I decided it must be done. I would write as much as I knew and could find out, hoping that at the end a book would materialize.

For months, I researched the 'Beverley Guardian' repeatedly, slowly building up my story. In many respects it was like a jigsaw puzzle, finding the bits to fit what I already knew, and gradually it began to take shape.

I hope my story will enable the reader to appreciate more fully the building in the corner of the Market Place known as 'The Home of Beautiful Pictures' — The Picture Playhouse.

'The Home of Beautiful Pictures' is published in celebration of British Film Year, 1985.

## ACKNOWLEDGEMENTS

This book would not have been possible without the enormous help and enthusiasm I have received from so many friends.

But my special thanks, in the first instance, must go to Mrs. Thelma Symmons, who kindly shared her many memories with me, passing on her first-hand experiences of the great number of years of her association with the Playhouse. I also appreciate the time taken in reading my manuscripts to maintain the accuracy of this publication.

My special thanks also go to Robert Curry, for I feel he had the hardest task of all, initially with research then trying to read and understand the enormous quantity of my hand-written manuscripts, then typing it repeatedly until it made sense. However, not just content at being involved with the early development of my book, Robert made another valuable contribution with his assistance in the critical and final edit before publication.

I am extremely grateful for the interest and enthusiasm shown by Charles Brook, Managing Director of the Hutton Press, for he has enabled 'The Home of Beautiful Pictures' to be another ambition fulfilled.

The 'Beverley Guardian' must be next, for they have been an invaluable source of reference in providing the backbone to my story, and in particular I thank Mr. Jeremy Ashcroft-Hawley, Editor of East Yorkshire Newspapers, for his kind permission in allowing me to quote and reproduce material.

I feel this is an appropriate place to thank Mr. Philip Brown and staff of the Beverley Public Library, for all their help and handling of the heavy and bound 'Beverley Guardians', and for being so patient with me when I requested the wrong year.

Two people I must certainly thank are Jon and Pat Gresham, for their interest in the Playhouse and for persuading me to become the Manager of same, thus fulfilling another ambition.

My appreciation and gratitude go to Nigel and Stella Spetch, who came to my rescue just as I had started to sink. I thank them both for their encouragement and also for the final typing of the manuscript. Thanks must also go to the following people: Richard Wilson, not just a friend to myself, but also a friend of the Playhouse, who has had our interests at heart for many years. I thank him for his encouragement and guidance with my story. Also to three members of the Playhouse staff who have made contributions to this story both directly and indirectly. Firstly, Paul Hesp, my thanks for his determination to see the Playhouse re-open as a cinema and during the period of transition his enthusiasm for the building which often put me to shame (and occasionally still does). Andrew Coverdale and Glen Jeffrey, both of whom joined the staff as the cinema re-opened and have supported me to date. Both Andrew and Glen have expressed tremendous interest in this publication, especially during the early stages when they made critical but constructive comments.

A friend of long-standing whom I dare not leave out is David Baldwin. Over ten years ago, when I discussed with him the possibility of writing a book about the Playhouse, we entered into a disagreement over the opening year of the Playhouse as a cinema. I would therefore take this opportunity to admit I was wrong, and am sorry to have kept you waiting so long for this apology — it's now official.

My list of acknowledgements isn't complete without mention of Professor Kidd. My thanks must go to the Professor, for it is his superb line-drawing of the Playhouse that has been used on the front cover of this publication.

I must also acknowledge the following sources of information that have made my story more interesting and complete. 'Remember Scarborough 1914' by David Mould, 'The History of Movie Photography' by Brian Coe, and the 'Guinness Book of Film Facts and Feats'.

Photographs and illustrated material in this publication have been taken from the author's private collection and are reproduced courtesy of Mrs. Thelma Symmons. Additional material has been used courtesy 'The Beverley Guardian' and the 'Hull Daily Mail'.

Every effort has been made to trace the copyright holders of material used in this publication. Should there be any omissions in this respect, we apologise and shall be pleased to make the appropriate acknowledgement in future editions.

P.H.R. March 1985.

# FOREWORD

Trying to find a suitably famous name to write what my Oxford English Dictionary defines as, 'introductory remarks, esp. by another than the author of the book', commonly known as a foreword, was the difficult task facing Peter Robinson when the time came to pen this page. In the end he gave up all hope of finding a 'name' and asked me to do the honours instead. Although I'd never written a foreword, and probably now never will again, I accepted the challenge and set to work.

Having bought the book you can now read it at your leisure, either forwards, backwards, from the middle or more adventurously upside down. It can be browsed through, used for reference or carefully scrutinized; you've paid for it so whatever you do with it is up to you. The book is presented in a chronological order, and if you decide to read it you may come across a particular section you enjoy more than any other, a name of someone you knew or know, or even a photograph which part- icularly impresses you so that you may want to show it to everyone you know. If you do then please mark the page with a bookmark as folding over page corners ruins a good book. You may on the other hand find it's not quite what you expected and that there's nothing of interest in it at all for you. This being the case you may be tempted to put the book in a drawer and forget about it. Please don't. It could be the correct thickness for propping up a table with a broken leg, or the correct weight to use as a doorstop or paperweight — either way other people will notice it and may take a look before rushing out to buy their own copy. Ideally, of course, you could leave it lying about on a table for your friends to browse through while you make coffee.

The photographs are used to enhance the text, and likewise, the text has been written to enhance the photographs. The layout is as simple as we could make it, and having been involved with the project since its inception (conception), I know just how much work has gone into the research to ensure the facts contained within are correct. It is a project of which Peter is particularly proud, and for myself I like to think that those days spent at the typewriter, and those evenings over a pint or two in local pubs have all been worth it and that I've been able to make a useful contribution. I have found it interesting, amusing and informative, and hope other readers will too. I also hope older readers will find it — if it's the correct term to use — nostalgic.

Many people who enter the building remark upon its beauty. The Picture Playhouse has a certain appeal to both young and old alike, and a quality that endears itself to you. The cinema is a popular place in the town, the attendance records prove that, and has, in one way or another, served the community for over 70 years. Let's hope it will continue to do so.

This book tells the story of The Picture Playhouse in words and pictures from 1911. It also tells the story of Ernest Symmons, the man who started it all when he saw a potential for motion pictures in Beverley, and a potential in the old Corn Exchange for showing them. To outline in more detail what you can expect to find within these pages would spoil the enjoyment of reading the book, and apart from that I've run out of space. So, enough of this rambling — you've read this far, now read on and take a journey through 'The Home of Beautiful Pictures'.

Robert Curry,

March 1985.

# INTRODUCTION

I don't think I could ever begin to assess the total number of hours I have spent at the Pictures over the years. My visits were, and still are, an occasion to me, and although I don't feel the same excitement now as I used to, it is still a great event.

From my early childhood, I have memories of being taken by my parents and an aunt to the pictures. My visits were frequent; evenings, Saturday mornings and afternoons. I didn't really mind what was showing – the more I went, the happier I was.

I devised my own 'moving picture show' using an old shoe box, newspaper photographs glued end to end and wound onto Grandma's meat skewers; then the kids next door would have to sit and watch as my pictures rolled by the aperture in the box. Of course, we had changes of programme, newspapers permitting (provided they didn't end up in the loo with a string through the corner first).

However, this did not fulfil my need for the real thing. I loved everything about the cinema: the smells, the torn tickets, and to me, the ultimate was a piece of film sometimes given free with chewing gum. These I really treasured.

One Christmas I was given a nursery rhyme slide projector. It would have been a real treat except that no one knew how to use it, and the whole family ended up peering down the lens. Thankfully, a Christmas Day visitor pointed us in the right direction – literally – and from then on our distempered walls became my screen.

A few Christmases later, moving pictures arrived in the form of my super new (second-hand) Pathé 9.5mm projector. I marvelled at those black and white moving pictures on the walls, and a wide choice of additional films listed in the Pathé catalogue were obtainable locally from Simson's photo/pet shop at Kemp's Corner which has long since moved and was developed into the property now occupied by the Leeds Permanent Building Society.

Although I was reasonably satisfied with my projector, I did like the looks of the Noris projector in Selles the Chemist window, and it was only £4–10–0 (£4–50). I gazed daily ensuring it was still there and saving desperately, but I never reached the target.

My visits to the real cinema continued as did my questions. I asked my father if, at the Marble Arch Cinema in Beverley, we saw the pictures before the people downstairs, because that balcony was so steep you could not see any audience below. I actually believed the pictures passed by on rollers like my newspaper pictures on meat skewers had done, and I thought we saw the pictures first because we had paid more to go upstairs. After all, we had climbed a lot of stairs!

Another question I asked was why did we nearly always see the end of the film first? This one I couldn't work out. The answer was because we were always going in at the end of the first performance, or as seats became available. I will never forget those long queues and the constant wondering whether we would get in or not, which added to the excitement of each wonderful occasion.

My earliest memories of what I saw on the Silver Screen go back to the Regal, and a film entitled "Rocket Ship X–M" (1950), which was all black and white until the landing on Mars when the picture became pink. I remember seeing Walt Disney's "Bambi" (1942) when I was about five years old – I think at the Marble Arch, but I'm not sure.

I wanted a Cinema of my own, but that was an impossible dream. I also had ambitions of becoming a cinema projectionist, but was soon advised by many that this was a job with no future. I can see that now, but at the time I argued the point bitterly.

I still had dreams of running a cinema even if I couldn't own one, and, as Manager of the Picture Playhouse, my ambitions to this extent have been fulfilled.

I like to reflect upon my cinemagoing and am reminded of the many times I was told that it wasn't healthy sitting for all those hours in those dark places when I should be out enjoying myself!!! But was my cinemagoing so different from the average TV or Video viewer of today? I think not.

Now to move on to the question of how I became so involved with the Playhouse. It all started with an aunt who would take my brother and I as a special treat to see Walt Disney films at the Playhouse, usually sitting in the best reserved seats, and if these were on the balcony it was even better especially if my school chums happened to look back at us from the cheaper seats at the front.

I can vaguely remember the proprietor, the late Mr Symmons, walking round and talking to people, some sitting in the rear stalls with rugs or blankets over their legs. I don't ever remember being cold in the Cinema, and even if I had been I don't think I was an important enough person to qualify for the blanket treatment.

Upon leaving school, I was fortunate enough to be employed as a school laboratory assistant, which required me to frequently call at the Playhouse to collect projector lamps and spare parts for a then newly established school audio/visual department, for which I was to become responsible, and as the Playhouse had the agency for Bell & Howell projectors and

Grundig tape recorders I welcomed the chance to call for lamps or other spares for the school's equipment. These visits gave me many chances to see behind the scenes and eventually afforded me the opportunity to earn much appreciated complimentary tickets for applying my artistic talents in producing advertising posters for a couple of shops in town.

All good things must come to an end as did the cinema side of the Playhouse in favour of bingo. I saw the Playhouse fill to capacity time and time again to the bingo caller's patter. I witnessed the bingo zenith and was still around for its demise.

During the bingo years there were times we thought we would lose our Playhouse when our landlord, the Beverley Borough Council, suggested alternative uses. Thankfully, our film society was to play an important part in saving the place from the big bad developers.

Our film society operated for nineteen seasons of six months each, and during those 9½ years provided a valauble service to the community in supplying film entertainment for the town again.

Well, the bingo players left to play their game elsewhere, so closure came and as the film society couldn't function as effectively anywhere else in the town, it too had to call time. This was not to be the end, however, for within just over three months of closure, films were to return to the Playhouse on a commercial basis, and I was invited to manage the (new) Playhouse Cinema.

I now feel that after so many years of my involvement with the Playhouse, I should make an attempt to record on paper her long and fine history of entertainment in Beverley, and at the same time pay tribute to the late Mr Ernest F. Symmons, for he made it the original "Home of Beautiful Pictures".

Over the many years I had made quite a few abortive attempts at putting on paper much of what I had committed to memory from stories told to me by Thelma Symmons and members of staff. I began to realise late in 1983 that I was an archive of Playhouse knowledge which I felt must be expanded, so with the encouragement of a friend, Robert Curry, I embarked upon a research project to fill in the gaps between what I already knew and what I thought you, the reader, would enjoy reading.

When I started the project I didn't think it was going to be too long a job, but I was soon to be proved wrong. I became fascinated with those old newspapers and cinema adverts and often lingered just a bit too long over some of them, photographing as many of them as I could afford, so I could study them at leisure.

Readers of my efforts who are familiar with the Playhouse and its people will, I fear, express concern over my omission of the very many staff and friends of the cinema over its many years of operation. I have to admit I purposely avoided mentioning too many past staff as I feel it would have detracted too much from my intention of writing about the Playhouse

Cinema and the man befind it. One person I must mention, however, is Ernest's son Brenton Symmons who passed away on December 31, 1983. Brenton was involved with the film industry for many years managing the Odeon at Harrogate until his retirement a few years ago. Brenton always had a tremendous affection for the Playhouse and its people, and this became very evident when he helped his step-mother, Thelma Symmons, fight the campaign to keep the Playhouse open during the early seventies.

On the many occasions I met Brenton, I could sense what I now know to be probably the strength of his father in him, especially when it came to his advice on running the Playhouse. I am sorry Brenton is not able to read my book, for I am sure he would have approved and welcomed it.

There are a few people to whom I must make special thanks here, as well as in my acknowledgements:

Mrs. Symmons who has been so patient reading and re-reading my manuscript, and, of course, keeping me right, for without her guidance I am afraid there would have been some quite substantial gaps in my story.

Robert Curry for his patience, and the great care with which he gave his invaluable help with research, typing, proof-reading and more typing, and his encouragement to keep me at it.

Mr. Philip Brown and the staff of the Beverley Public Library, who I'm sure must have got fed up handling and carrying those year-at-a-time bound 'Beverley Guardians' covering the period of my research.

Stella and Nigel Spetch who came to my rescue with help just when I needed it.

Richard Wilson for his expert guidance and encouragement.

I think that's about all I have to say except that I've done my best with the writings and although I feel it's more like a catalogue of Playhouse Happenings I do hope you enjoy it. Please forgive any omissions or inaccuracies that may have occurred. Perhaps your own memories could provide the basis for a second book, 'Playhouse Remembered?'.

# CHAPTER 1

## Moving Pictures Come To Beverley

Paris, December 28th, 1895. The Lumiere brothers made their first presentation to the paying public of their Cinematograph moving pictures.

Two years later, on January 18th, 1897, what is believed to be the first moving picture show to the paying public of Beverley took place at the Assembly Rooms, presented by the Beverley Photographic and Sketching Society, who, at great expense, engaged Mr. Birt Acres to give his 'wonderful and startling performance with the Royal Cinematescope, or Animated Photographs (as exhibited at Marlborough House with great success on the eve of the Royal Wedding)'. This demonstration of animated photographs was welcomed by a large and very enthusiastic audience, the large Assembly Room being crowded.

The Reverend Canon Nolloth, D.D., was in the chair and as Vice-President of the society introduced Mr. Acres who went on to give an account of his experiments over a period of twenty years leading up to his invention of the Cinematescope. The animated photographs had been taken on half-inch wide transparent film by Mr. Acres, and with the aid of a lantern were magnified 6,000 times!

Just over 14 years after the Royal Cinematescope, Ernest Frederick Symmons and partner Leslie C. Holderness presented to the paying public the 'Imperator' Cinematograph pictures in the Corn Exchange, Beverley.

Beverley is an historic market town which has some very beautiful and interesting buildings, the Minster and St. Mary's churches being without doubt the most magnificent. With its old streets and unique charm, Beverley, like York, has always attracted people with artistic ability and interests. Ernest Symmons was one such person.

One prominent, although not beautiful, building full of Victorian dignity and character was the Corn Exchange nestling in a corner of the Saturday Market. Built in 1886 at a cost 'not to exceed £2,000' and comprising a Corn Exchange, Public Bath and Butter Market, with Porters' accommodation and Engine House, the Corn Exchange and Butter Market had to be arranged so as to form one large public room when required!

This was the place that proved of great interest to Ernest and his partner, resulting in a letter dated January 24th, 1911, applying for the use of the Corn Exchange for the exhibition of Cinematograph pictures. Thanks to the help of Councillor Robert Hammond, the Corn Exchange and Butter

Market, together with part of the Baths, were let to Messrs Debenham & Co., of York for a period of three months from February 20th, 1911 at a rent of £5 per week. This agreement was to herald regular exhibitions of the new and very popular moving pictures in the town for many years ahead.

The opening performance on Feburary 20th, 1911 was advertised as a 'high class programme at popular prices, 6d, 4d, 2d,' and contained 'pictures of interest and humour', a beautiful coloured Pathé film entitled, 'A Drama of 200 years Ago', and such topical gems as 'The Opening of Parliament by King George V' and 'Bird Nesting on Flamboro' Head'. With twice nightly performances, 'popular prices', and 'excellent programmes', the press also felt confident that full houses would follow!

Many people may not realise that at the time of the Cinematograph's arrival in Beverley, the town had no electricity. It was to be many years before electricity became available to the town, mainly because the Council owned the Gas Works and were not too enthusiastic over its introduction. However, electricity was to become available to those who wanted it from September 25th, 1930. This meant that anyone wanting power had to generate it themselves. This was the problem facing the two proprietors of the Corn Exchange. The immediate solution to the lack of electricity was the installation of a Pelapone petrol and paraffin engine. This was started with petrol then run on paraffin.

The eight-cylinder engine wasn't without problems. Being water-cooled it frequently 'furred up' without warning, and if this happened during a performance it was a case of cash refund or tickets for a future show. The proprietors had been known to work throughout the night stripping down the engine, de-furring the cylinders and re-assembling before the next show could go on. These problems were to continue until about 1918 when a more reliable and efficient Gas Engine was installed — this didn't sieze up, but it did require two men to swing the gigantic flywheel!

With their own ' Electricity Plant' providing their power needs, the 'High Class Programmes' could be presented at their best, especially with the use of the latest 'Imperator' projector which offered 'steady and flickerless' pictures of quality projected onto an eighteen-foot screen.

Within a month of opening, the 'Beverley Guardian' made favourable comments stating that the Cinematograph exhibitions were 'the best that have been seen in the town, and those who had not yet paid a visit, and are desirous of spending a pleasant evening, should lose no time in doing so.' According to the 'Beverley Guardian' of March 18th, 1911, 'the pictures are the best that can be obtained, and the room has been most comfortably arranged, and absolute safety of the audience is guaranteed, the engine and entire apparatus being separated from the room by a brick wall, through a small aperture in which the Pictures are shown on the screen.' So well patronised were the exhibitions, that within only four months the proprietors applied for an extension to the period of their tenancy.

Having now established the success of Cinematograph Exhibitions in Beverley, allow me to introduce you to the people behind these developments.

Ernest Frederick Symmons was born on July 14th, 1882, the son of a draper who had businesses in Boscombe and Bournemouth. Ernest's father had artistic talents and, possibly 'like father like son', saw this potential in him, for at the age of 16, the young Ernest was apprenticed to the Stereoscopic Co., in Regent Street, London. Seven years later, he qualified as a professional portrait photographer and moved north, setting up a business in Clifford Street, York. Known as Debenham and Company, it was eventually to become very well known and accepted in the film industry.

Although portrait photography continued to provide exceptionally good business, the new and novel moving pictures were soon to become of increasingly great interest to Ernest. Shortly after marrying in 1908, Ernest Symmons formed a partnership with his brother-in-law, Leslie Holderness. Ernest and Leslie were to become the first regular Cinematograph exhibitors in Beverley and sole proprietors of the Corn Exchange. Their partnership was to last only until 1919 when Lt. L.C. Holderness (Royal Scots Greys) returned from the war and eventually took up a position with a London cinema.

The 'film-going' public of Beverley 'greatly approved' of the new-fangled entertainment provided by the partners, and a request for a two-year lease was made to the Council. In those early days, a year in film terms lasted only eight months, ceasing operations at the end of May or early June around the time of the first Beverley Race Meeting. This break allowed musicians to fulfil their summer contracts. In the application for this extension, a request was also made for the removal of two substantial pillars from the centre of the hall. Approval was given and the pillars were eventually removed. A continuing stipulation of the terms of the lease was that films could not be exhibited on Saturdays between 2.00 and 4.30 p.m. as this was the time the Corn Market was in operation.

During my researches, I frequently found references to Fox Hunting films. Obviously these were very popular, the earliest being in March 1911 when the film, 'Fox Hunting' came to Beverley. It was advertised as, 'one of the greatest London successes, and people are flocking in thousands to see it'. A reviewer of the day described the film, as, 'one of the most wonderful things yet accomplished by the Cinematograph'.

Without doubt the subject must have been popular, for within the same programme, Mr. Uriah Butters presented a number of lantern slides he had taken of the Holderness Hunt! Not only did Mr. Butters take lantern slides of these events, but Ernest advertised that, if fine, he proposed taking Cinematograph film in the Market Place of the meet of the Holderness Hounds, and all interesting local events connnected with the meet. He urged that the public look for his camera. He stated the night the film would be screened and advised reservation of seats for the 'Special Hunt Night'.

In September 1911, the first summer break was over and the Corn Exchange re-opened as 'The Picture Playhouse'. The press reported the success of the previous season and announced that some 'very fine programmes' had been secured. The re-opening programme would contain film of King George V's Coronation, and an eye-witness report of the actual pageant announced that this film was 'a great triumph of the Cinematograph art'.

The re-opening press review in the 'Beverley Guardian' told readers that, 'during the season the proprietors will be Cinematographing some local events in Beverley, and the Citizens of this town will be enabled to see themselves on the screen 'as others see them'. With his new cinema, a ready outlet for Ernest's films awaited.

He soon became a very popular figure in the community. Being especially distinguished by his large tripod and motion picture camera, he was seen often to frequent the town's industries and schools to record the townsfolk leaving work and school. One can easily imagine the tremendous excitement of being filmed ' to see themselves as others see them'. Of course, these events were advertised, and with such titles as, 'Men Leaving the Tanyard', and, 'Children Leaving School', how many people in 1911 could resist the temptation of seeing themselves in moving pictures?

An attraction during the opening year was the first 'Beverley Children Beauty Contest' offering a first prize of a 'crisp £5 note', a second prize of a silver wristlet watch valued at one guinea, and five other prizes of silver brooches each worth half a guinea. With such attractive prizes and the chance of seeing your baby in moving pictures, a tremendous amount of interest was generated in the town. To enter the contest, all one had to do was submit an original photograph which would be considered by a committee of well-known gentlemen in their quest for the 'prettiest and healthiest' children. Once selected, the children were filmed in fancy dress with their pets (if applicable) and the film screened for the audience to judge. A rather interesting voting system was operated. 1/- (5p) seat holders were entitled to six votes, 6d (2½p) to three votes, 4d (1½p) to two votes, and 2d (1p) to one vote, but if you came to 'Early Doors' you got one extra vote! Each evening the votes would be counted and the results displayed outside the cinema. It takes little imagination to guess what happened. On noting the position on each new list of their little ones, the relatives and friends were rounded up to go and vote for the favoured child, and, if neccessary, go in and pay for their seats over and over again on the same night in order to win more votes. I do not know who the winners were, but the lucky contestants were presented with their prizes by Mrs. David Nutchey, wife of Councillor Nutchey, and after the award ceremony, the film was cut up and each mother was presented with a portion bearing her child's photo. The whole contest was reported by the 'Beverley Guardian' to have attracted very large houses.

As 1911 drew to a close, the Playhouse celebrated its first Christmas. Music came with a selection of Christmas tunes played on the harp by Ernest's partner, Leslie Holderness, carol singing was presented as a contest for children, and on the screen Thomas Alva Edison's film version of the Charles Dickens classic, 'A Christmas Carol' (1911) provided a special treat for the inmates of the workhouse, who had been invited to see the film. A present of an ounce of tobacco was given to all the 'old men', this being donated by Mr. Turner, a local tobacconist, while the women were all given packets of sweets by Mrs. Holderness, wife of Leslie.

Within the tenancy agreement, the Corporation had to provide suitable chairs and forms, the latter being purchased at 1/9 (9p) and 2/3 (11p) per foot. No doubt the 2/3 ones were guaranteed to be splinterless. Curtains were provided at a cost of £9/11/0 (£9.55) and, if the Corn Market objected to them, the Corporation would have to put up blinds to stop the light. The technical classes that had used the Playhouse would have to use the Baths during the closed season and Debenham and Co. were asked to contribute £10 towards the £25 cost of boarding over the baths to accommodate the classes. If the arrangement failed then Debenham and Co. should, at their own expense, provide alternative accommodation.

To anyone unfamiliar with The Playhouse I feel mention must be made of the large amounts of glass within the building, not just side windows, but in the roof, and throughout the years light has caused many problems especially on bright sunny days. However, in late 1911 the problem wasn't too much light but, according to Corn Merchants having stands in the Corn Exchange, insufficient illumination because the glass lights in the roof had been blacked out with paper pasted on them. They made the request 'to have the Exchange made suitable for its original purpose'. The solution was simple. The council fitted new blinds in place of the pasted papers.

Another grumble against the new 'Cinematograph Entertainment' came from the Girls' Swimming Sports Committee. As well as moaning about the overall inadequacy of the Public Baths, they were far from happy with the reduction of space brought about by the Cinematograph engine being installed within the Baths area. The poor Baths accommodation was to be a subject discussed for over sixty years, with many references being made to the use of the Playhouse to extend the Baths. Fortunately, with a firm decision for the placement of the new town Baths in the early 1970's, this threat was permanently alleviated.

On April 6th, 1912, there came the announcement that the proprietors of the Playhouse were to attempt something never before done in Beverley. They planned to make a local comic film with acting contributions from a number of local celebrities. Further announcements would be made from the 'platform' that evening. The film was made and entitled, 'Professor Swizzle, F.I.B.,' and showed the professor's adventures

17

in Beverley on Easter Monday. The professor had invented a special powder 'which blows out of sight anything upon which he turns it'. The powder was used to dispense with a ticket collector, cab fares and other 'petty annoyances'. The professor went on to use the powder with amazing effect in different parts of the town, like blowing the Bellman 'sky high' after which he fell victim of his own invention and was blown into space. [1]

In September 1912, with summer over and the promise of dark nights ahead, the moving pictures returned to the town. In the 'Beverley Guardian' for September 30th, an advertisement appeared for cinema shows in the Assembly Rooms (eventually to become the Regal Cinema). This was the 'Electric Cinema Picture Palace'. The general manager of the circuit was Judge Bolton and they proudly announced that 'every picture is the best and up to date', with one house nightly and programme changes Monday and Thursday at popular prices, 2d (1p), 4d (1½p), 6d (2½p), 1/- (5p). [2]

As the Playhouse re-opened after its summer break, patrons were, on entering, greeted with the sight of a few improvements. Firstly, the two pillars in the centre, which had impeded the view of the screen for so many had been removed. A sloping floor had been installed at the rear and, at considerable expense, to add further to the comfort of the patrons, the back of the hall had been re-seated with tip-up plush chairs of the best quality. Those seats had been made specially to order, being larger and broader than the usual seats.

Another improvement was the installation of the latest thing in Cinematograph Projectors called the 'Indomitable'. This was the same make of machine that had, in 1912, received the highest approval of His Majesty, King George V when at Cowes on the Isle of Wight. He had particularly asked to see the projector and complimented the British makers on having invented the steadiest and most flickerless machine he had yet seen.

As a change from the nightly film programme, one Tuesday in October 1912 the Playhouse was loaned to the Literary and Scientific Society for their opening meeting. The lecture was given by Mr. K. Kearton on, 'Bioscoping Big Game in Africa', and was well illustrated by cinematograph lantern slides which were shown by the proprietors of the Playhouse.

[1] I got the impression that this comic film was probably great fun to make, especially for the onlooker, for I doubt if they could or would understand what was going on. Obviously, stop-motion photography would be used for the disappearing sequences, whereby an actor or object is filmed in front of the camera which is then stopped, the subject removed, and filming re-commenced. On the projected film, the subject just disappears. In 1912 this must have amazed audiences.

[2] In my researches I have not discovered much relating to the 'Electric Cinema', although in 1913 I came across a headline in the 'Beverley Guardian' which caught my eye: 'Cinematograph Operator in Trouble'. I read on with great interest. Apparently, Leonard Heenan, who was the operator of the 'Electric Cinema' in the Assembly Rooms had been charged with being drunk and disorderly, and with using bad language! He admitted to being ashamed of himself and 'felt his position very much'. He was fined 10/- (50p).

The evening was very successful with the Playhouse almost full.

November brought announcements that the proprietors had invented a new screen which would greatly enhance the beauty of the cinematograph pictures. They went on to say that the Playhouse would be the first hall to see the results of their experiments. [3]

December brought a children's beauty competition, with the first prize of £5 going to Ethel and Jessie, the twin daughters of Mr. B. W. Whinnerah of Longcroft. 'The prizes were very gracefully presented to the winners by Councillor Mrs. David Nutchey.'

During these early years the moving pictures were often supported by other outstanding attractions. On one occasion, not only were 'Three entire changes of programme' advertised in one week, but Miss Lily May gave a clever exhibition of skipping rope dancing with orchestral accompaniment. Further 'outstanding attractions' included, 'special musical items' when several ladies came from York to sing, and a 'Sacred Concert' featuring the Minster Quartette of Beverley.

I was surprised to discover Christmas Day openings, sometimes with matinees, although no 'comic' films were shown. I understand these Christmas shows never did much business, even with a Christmas attraction like Miss Gertrude Pagan who performed two of the latest dances at each performance on Christmas and Boxing days. Gertrude Pagan was a young, pretty and talented dancer, a protege of a well-known Beverley artistic lady, Miss Madge Whiting and her brother, the architect, Richard Whiting, who lived in Hengate opposite the White Horse Inn, known as 'Nellie's'. (Richard was the donor of the first White Horse sign over the front door of the inn, which, according to local legend, was his nursery rocking horse). It was Richard who drew up the plans for the balconies at the Playhouse. Unfortunately, no planning permission had been obtained before they were built, and the Beverley Corporation showed their displeasure by withdrawing the Cinema Licence for three months.

Occasionally, programmes would last over two hours, some being advertised as 'long and varied' or 'you will enjoy this long programme', commencing at 7.00 and finishing at 10.15. If you found those forms a bit hard and you had the cash, then comfort awaited you in the 'reserved seats' (tip-up plush chairs) for one shilling (5p).

During May 1914 the film '60 Years a Queen' was shown. School children were invited to enter a competition. They were to write an essay about the film. Nearly 300 entries were received, making it a most 'difficult matter to decide which were the best'. The Mayor (Mr. M. M. Westerby) kindly presented the prizes given by the 'enterprizing proprietors' of the Playhouse for the ten best essays. The prizes were vouchers for five shillings (25p) — so that the children could choose their own prize to that

[3] Unfortunately I cannot trace any more information on this screen, or its installation.

value from local tradesmen. A 'brilliant' essay had come from Lillian Clayton who obtained full marks out of a possible twenty. A special mention was made of little six year old Raymond Howes who took on a 'collossal' task of writing three pages of foolscap. Also worth mentioning are two amusing sentences from two of the younger entrants: One said, 'Queen Victoria had had four children and then she had a baby'; the other was, 'After Queen Victoria died she was turned into a statue'.

As the new entertainment gathered momentum and gained greater popularity, a 'substantial' lease of three years was granted to the tenants of the Playhouse. This success encouraged by the enthusiasm of Ernest and his local pictures, regardless of subject, must have exerted an impressionable influence on the picture-going public of the day.

During these pioneering days the availability of laboratories for film processing was very scant, and speed was one of the first essentials for any news item. After filming, for example, a Saturday event, Ernest would rush off on his A.J.S. Motorcycle, complete with sidecar, to York, where he would process and title the film and have it complete for screening on Monday night, much to the delight of eager audiences.

June 26th, 1914 saw the recording of another important newsreel. This was the opening of The King George Dock in Hull by King George V and Queen Mary. Tragically, like so many of the early films, time has taken its toll and now only a mere two minutes of the film has survived showing this great occasion. However, amidst a mass of scratches and blemishes on the film, their Majesties can still clearly be seen.

At 8.00 a.m. on the morning of Wednesday, December 16th, 1914, six German battleships appeared out of the mist to deliver a shattering raid along the East Coast; their targets were Scarborough, Whitby and Hartlepool. The attack shocked the nation. It had come only four months from the outbreak of hostilities.

Scarborough was completely unprotected, and had neither guns nor ships to defend herself with. During the half hour the bombardment lasted, over 500 shells fell on Scarborough causing the deaths of 124, and injuries to 500, including a Beverley man, Private Leo Bulman, who was seriously wounded when he was struck by shrapnel and received severe injuries to ankles, thighs, wrist and head. After a long struggle crawling to safety, the first thing he asked for was a cigarette. Private Bulman was a recruit with the reserve battalion of the 5th A.P.W.O. York Regiment (Territorials). He had enlisted only six weeks previously and had gone to Scarborough to guard the electric power station. The damage was incredible. Schools, churches, shops, homes, all were affected. The Grand Hotel proved an easy target, being hit by 36 shells causing an estimated £13,000 worth of damage.

Up the coast at Whitby their bombardment lasted, thankfully, for only eleven minutes, but even in that time over 150 shells fell damaging about 30 buildings causing the deaths of three people and injuring a further three.

At Hartlepool as the German ships attacked, so they came under fire from shore batteries and a naval patrol; even with the shore defences the death toll reached 102 with 449 injuries.

Newspapers carried stories of this appalling raid on their front pages attempting to convey the effects of the real horror felt by those most affected, but probably the greatest impact was depicted in the Newsreel film made by Ernest showing the results of the outrage. It takes little imagination to realise the impact on the cinema-going public this film would have. Part of this film still survives, and although much the worse for wear, the remaining footage shows the extensive damage to property. One scene, very recognisable, shows Scarborough lighthouse with a substantial hole in the tower. So bad was this damage that it had to be demolished.

As I browsed through a few worn and aged programmes from those early years I came across one announcement from the proprietors regarding their rights to alter the programme and order of films when necessary, thus disclaiming responsibility for not showing the advertised films. The reason was quite clear — Railway Delays. This reminded me of an amusing story I once heard, and no doubt it happened many times, which tells of an occasion when the programme was late arriving, so Ernest stood in front of the audience and apologised for the delay, but as the films were expected at any minute he would show them (yet again) 'Queen Victoria's Funeral'! (This announcement being greeted with groans). Printed in one programme I found this little gem: 'All good things come to them who wait', and what more appropriate for a delayed programme?

For just over five years film entertainment in Beverley had been unchallenged. However, this was to change when, on September 16th, 1916, competition for the Picture Playhouse came with the opening of The Marble Arch Picture Palace in Butcher Row. This was a luxury custom built cimema with a seating capacity of 1,100 and boasting a 'charming room on the first floor, where there is a commodious and thoroughly up-to-date cafe'. The Playhouse couldn't boast anything to match this, but it did have one important factor to continue its success, Ernest Symmons, and his tremendous enthusiasm and showmanship. The local newsreels continued to include such popular items as the 'Meeting of the Hounds', 'Baby Shows', 'Local Weddings' and events like 'The Royal Flying Corps' Sports'. These were the subjects that kept the audiences going to the Playhouse.

I was surprised to discover that not all films of this period had a general appeal. When the film 'The Despoiler' (1916) was to be exhibited at the Playhouse it was advertised as 'intended for men and women only'. Further research did not reveal any reason for this restriction, but what I did discover was 'The Despoiler' had been viewed in private by 'several gentlemen of the town who considered it a masterpiece'! Regardless of the restrictive viewing the total box-office take (less entertainment tax) was donated to the 'Victory War Loan' funds.

June 1917, saw the offer of another crisp £5 note as the first prize for the bonniest war baby. To qualify, the baby had to have been born in '1914 and since that time'. A second prize of £2, and third prize of £1, were also offered for this competition of which the 'conditions are most simple'. The patrons were given voting papers to record their votes on, and, of course, 'no favouritism can be shown by the management as the public are the judge'.

After the contest, the film was cut up, thus enabling each parent to be 'the proud possessor of an animated picture of their little ones'.

Throughout the 1914-18 War, the public were constantly reminded of the need to exercise the law on the efficient use of blackout. One public announcement I found read as follows: 'In the event of an Air Raid Alarm being received, all lights within the borough must be extinguished, lights of every description including the striking of matches will be prohibited'. It was signed by order of the Chief Constable.

This allows me to introduce an interesting story I found in the 'Beverley Guardian'. The incident occured on the night of March 12th, 1918 'in a case of sudden emergency'. John W. Laughton, a butcher of the Market Place, had come on duty as a Special Constable about 7.30 p.m., and had found 'light reflecting' from the Playhouse entrance door. He told the attendant on duty at the cinema that an alarm had been given, at the same time requesting that the door be kept closed. Ten minutes later Special Constable Laughton again noticed the light showing, so he rang the Chief Constable.

The Chief Constable (Mr. Carpenter), upon receiving the message from Special Constable Laughton, immediately phoned the Playhouse and told the young lady who answered that the lights must be attended to. After this warning the lights were alleged to have been extinguished. However, Walter Evans, boot dealer of the Market Place and a Special Constable, had seen the light showing at about 7.30 p.m., again at 8.00 and then at 9.00.

Bernard Stephenson, hosier, and John Dean, gardener, both Special Constables, claimed they saw the light at 9 o'clock.

Later, in court, Ernest said he had always endeavoured to carry out the instructions or orders of the police. After his secretary had told him of the Chief Constable's 'phone call he took out all the electric light bulbs and also let down a curtain from the roof to the door, which excluded any light which might come from inside the hall. On the night in question, two Special Constables had rushed into the building. One of them shouted: 'For God's sake, stop the show and put the lights out'. To put the hall in total darkness could have resulted in a serious accident. At this time Ernest had received no instruction from the Chief Constable to stop the show and 'thought it was only right to carry on as in the past'. Mr. J. R. Lane, the witness for the defence, said that between 8.00 and 8.15 he had 'found the place quite in darkness', and P. C. Liberty who said that when, at 7.45, he asked the young lady to put out the two lights in front she had done so, and later Mr. Symmons took out the electric bulbs.

Evelyn Jenney, a cash taker at the Playhouse, said that when the Specials complained, all the lights were extinguished except a small light in the paybox which was shaded. Another witness, Fred Boyes, said that just before 9 o'clock, two Specials rushed into the hall and and shouted: 'Get those lights out' nearly causing a panic.

Thelma Monsen, secretary, said she had received the message from the Chief Constable to 'Please keep the door closed as there had been complaints'. She denied that the message was that the lights must be extinguished.

In summing up, Mr. Tom Turner of the police court said that on the evidence of the Special Constables, which 'had not been touched in any way whatever', they were bound to convict, and there would be a fine imposed of £2.

With the War over by almost a year, 1919 brought the novel and 'high class' Musical Item Competition, and with such outstanding prizes as First: £50, Second: £30, and Third: £5, plus other cash prizes, what musician could fail to be attracted?

The volume of applause was to decide the winners with 'Three independent Gentlemen placed in different parts of the Hall' to judge the applause. The competitor who received the greatest applause on any of the entry nights went on to compete in the semi-finals and then the final, where the judging was again by applause and marks awarded by the two Honorary Musical Judges, Mr. J. Camidge, M.A., Mus. B(ac)., F.R.C.O., (Organist Beverley Minster), and Mr. Malkin, F.R.C.O., A.R.C.M., L. Mus., T.C.L. Competitors had to appear in evening, uniform or fancy dress. They could use their own name or be known by a pseudonym, appear masked and incognito. All this entertainment, in addition to the full and complete picture programme, was to be over in time for the 'Competitors to catch the last train to Hull'.

Ernest Symmons and his Picture Playhouse had for quite some time been noted for helping various charities, and, as I have discovered, Ernest's generosity was well remembered by many. The Beverley Cottage Hospital was one of the major benefactors of Ernest's efforts, with probably the most popular fund raiser being the Sunday Concert with all proceeds donated to the 'Cottage Hospital Radio Fund to provide the extra wireless equipment'. Whatever the cause, if it was worthy, Ernest was there with any help possible. Besides concerts, music played a very important part in the enjoyment of the Silent Cinema. I am told the musicians could make or break a film. Their necessity was possibly what appeared to make them such a temperamental lot! One Musical Director of the Playhouse, a certain Madame Nellie Gibbons, would insist on having a coffee break with biscuits during the interval in the office. 'Madame' appeared to have a nasty habit of creating very long and involved conversations, known on occasions to extend to an hour! As can be appreciated this was much to the annoyance of the patrons and staff, but who dared to upset such an important person? One person who did get upset was a pianist who was often baited by the children, until one night someone hurled a tomato at him which squashed on impact. Upon receipt of same the pianist immediately ceased playing, closed and locked the piano, and walked away with the key, never to be seen again.

Mrs. Symmons assures me it was common practice in those days to eat anything in the cinema, this being recognisable from the rubbish left behind; pea-pods, prawn heads and tails, plus assorted bits of fruit and vegetable, so for the odd occasion when a missile was needed there was almost always something at hand.

With fox hunting being a very popular sport, especially in the East Riding of Yorkshire, Ernest after much thought decided to make a 'feature' film about it. This involved going out on many cold, wet and windy days on motorbike and sidecar, following horses, riders and hounds.

He acquired some really excellent shots of the Holderness Hunt taken at various points on their many days out, but he desperately needed some 'fill in' shots of the fox!

Ernest let it be known that he would give £5 to anyone bringing him a fox, tame or wild, and eventually a local game keeper arrived with a fox, which was tethered to a post on a long lead. The long shots obtained of the 'hunted fox' helped to make 'Fox Hunting' a very attractive film.

The musical score by the then well-known musical director Freddie Kitchen of the Majestic Cinema, Leeds, made a major contribution to the film's success, which had audiences 'riding' in their seats. Although not confirmed, I understand Ernest sold 'Fox Hunting' for £2,000, quite a sum of money in those days.

Ernest also produced a series of films, which, on their national release, were advertised as a 'special attraction'. These were made for 'Famous Films', and titled 'Modern Dances and How to do Them', which, as the title implies, were demonstrations of the popular dances of the day, to quote the advance publicity for the series 'Picturized by England's leading exponents of the Art' Gertrude Pagan and C. Stevenson. Popular as they were one reviewer wrote that they were 'lacking in quality and rhythm'!

I feel now is the time to introduce you to a young lady who was to rapidly become a very important person within the Picture Playhouse and the life of Ernest. She was Miss Thelma Monsen, who eventually was to become the second Mrs. Symmons and be responsible for running the business for many years.

Miss Thelma Monsen was first introduced to Ernest and the Playhouse in 1916 by her father who was a seaman and had known Ernest for some time. Thelma's father asked Ernest to keep an eye on his family should anything happen to him when he returned to sea. Tragically, he was killed almost immediately.

Miss Monsen, who thankfully had learnt shorthand and typing, asked Ernest about getting a job at the Playhouse. As he and his partner, Leslie Holderness, worked alternate nights, this smart young lady gave the impression of being able to work for two bosses without much effort and was taken on.

After a couple of years Thelma was practically running the business, doing almost everything except signing the cheques; she also became involved with frequent coverage of newsreel events often helping to carry equipment and films. Thelma was to pove her worth in this respect when, on August 24th, 1921, at 5.40 p.m., the R38 Airship from Howden slowly sailed over the fascinated crowds watching in Hull's Old Town. Suddenly, without warning, this 695 foot long monster broke in half, plunging into the River Humber below. Forty-six people perished, leaving only five survivors.

At the time Thelma Monsen was in Hull's Station Square on her way to catch the Beverley train, and seeing the Airship break up and hearing someone say it had gone down in the Humber she had to let Ernest know, but as he wouldn't arrive in Beverley Station from York until 6.17 Thelma went on ahead. Arriving at Beverley she waited for his train. On arrival no time was wasted in getting to Hull. Fortunately he had a camera and film with him, and Thelma accompanied him.

Arriving at the Humber, Ernest approached a man with a small boat requesting his help with the aid of a £5 note. The man took him out to the wreckage of the gigantic illfated Airship where film was taken before the tide covered it, making the film of great value.

The unprocessed film was sent straight on to the Pathé Fréres Company in London, who paid Ernest the magnificent sum of £50. It is interesting to note that part of this film was included in two film documentaries during the 1970's, 'Death in the Sky' and 'Havoc', the latter having a world wide television distribution.

Musical treats became a speciality of many cinemas during the silent era, musical or vocal renditions being part of the evening's entertainment. The Playhouse was no exception, offering 'Special music by the Picture Playhouse Trio', or another occasion in addition to the usual programme was 'Special Violin Recitals by the noted Russian Violinist Effin Libine, The Great Artist' or the cinema's very own Miss Thelma Monsen who made her vocal debut singing 'Smilin' Through' and went on to become a star attraction. Unfortunately, Thelma's excellent and trained voice was not to be heard as frequently as the patrons would have liked, because due to a chest condition her singing career was soon ended. However, I feel sure Thelma will be remembered with affection by many for her vocal presentations at the Playhouse.

One film of Ernest's received overseas distribution. This was an advertising film about Hull, showing the Docks and Industries at work.

This 'propaganda' film was sponsored by the North Eastern and Hull and Barnsley Railway Companies and did a grand tour of Australia, New Zealand, South Africa and Canada.

A press review reported that the film took three months to make during the winter, 'The worst possible period for open-air cinema work', but despite this a 'remarkable' film was made. At the press showing of the film 'The Picture was shown at a more rapid rate than usual, but took three quarters of an hour in the showing'.

I found this review amusing as there was no indication as to why the film should be shown at a more 'rapid rate' than the usual 16 frames per second.

From industry to country lanes, the smell of the woodlands, and the wind upon the purple heather. If this was for you then Ideal Films would know that you would appreciate their 'Home and Beauty Series' of 'Gems of the Picturesque North'.

These were a series of short travel films of about 800 feet in length made by Ernest in conjunction with the North Eastern Railway Company. Each film showed familiar scenes of places like Bridlington, Whitby, York, Harrogate, and a Train Ride from Whitby to Pickering, (plus many more, as listed in the appendix under 1921). 'Gems of the Picturesque North' claimed to be different from most other 'scenics', being full of 'variety and life' with photography of a 'high order' depicting scenes of the 'Mother Land' and 'answering a real want in the cinema world'. Although extensive researches have been carried out in an attempt to trace these films produced during the 1920's, to date I have been unsuccessful.

Ernest Symmons was fortunate in negotiating deals for many popular and very successful films for the Playhouse. I have been told by Thelma Symmons of the 'enormous' business experienced for the exhibition of 'The Sheik' (1921 Dir: George Melford) starring Rudolph Valentino.

'The Sheik' had been playing to 'utmost capacity' in the big cities, and this was the story repeated at the Playhouse. Never had so many people queued to see a film; the market place was 'packed', and as the 'House Full' sign went up for the 6.30 show so the next full house was waiting outside for the 8.45.

The box office opened twice daily, 11.00 to 1.00 and 2.00 to 4.00, for advance bookings and with no increased seat prices for this 'costly production'.

Preceding the film Tom Booth (Baritone), a pupil of Victor Gigaunun, Brussels Conservatoire sang specially arranged Eastern songs, and to create just the right atmosphere Ernest had designed a beautiful Eastern scene, the whole set being illuminated by an amazing electrical lighting creation.

Did you know that cinema shows operated on long-distance trains at one time, just as they do on aeroplanes today? I have an interest in railways as well as the cinema and remember reading a book entitled 'Railways in the

Cinema', by John Huntley (the interested reader is directed to this fascinating work), and while reading it I came across an entry for 'The Railway Centenary' Kinomatographed by Debenham and Co., York. This referred to a film produced by Ernest in 1925 of the 'Darlington Railway Centenary'. Fortunately I was able to buy a copy of this historic steam parade, the film also showing the Duke and Duchess of York who were present at the event.

Reluctant as I am to make critical comment I did find the camera-positions rather unimaginative for the subject. However, the film was screened at the Playhouse and received high praises, including one from Japan which according to a press report read 'The Japanese Government have placed a high value on this picture and have secured a copy of it for their countrymen to see'.

Throughout these early years of entertainment at the Playhouse, the corn chandling had continued. Each Saturday the merchants met to conduct their transactions, which meant that each Friday night at least 100 seats had to be removed and then re-fixed again each Saturday tea-time ready for the evening performance. This problem was solved in 1927 when the merchants moved to the Cattle Market, much to the relief of the cinema staff.

During 1927 not only did you see Constance Talmadge in her best film 'The Duchess of Buffalo' (1926, Dir: Sidney Franklin) but you could join in the Community Singing under the direction of Miss Elsa Gow, L.T.C.L., for a good half hour before the big picture, and judging by the number of advertisements, Community Singing was certainly very popular during that year.

Another attraction was a film of Beverley Races taken by Ernest and what appears to have been an almost annual event, the Territorials in Camp on Westwood, although I cannot find more details of these films.

As mentioned earlier, not all films had a 'general' appeal, especially with one 'Intended for Men and Women only', for I came across another film, 'Dawn', (1928 Dir: Herbert Wilcox) which had been banned by the film censor. All was not lost for Beverley audiences however, because the Beverley Magistrates and Chief Constable viewed the film and gave permission for the Picture Playhouse to screen it, with two special matinees arranged to 'enable invalids and those living outside Beverley to witness 'Dawn'.

*Ernest Frederick Symmons, Founder of the Playhouse Cinema.*

*Early print of the Corn Exchange.*

# EAST RIDING ADVERTISER.
### IS INCORPORATED THE EAST RIDING TELEGRAPH.

[Price One Penny.]

REGISTERED AT THE G.P.O. AS A NEWSPAPER.

SATURDAY, FEBRUARY 18, 1911.

...ANY, JOHN V. NUTCHEY, SOLE PROPRIETOR, BEVERLEY,

...es' Celebrated Cultivators, Ploughs, Diggers, Self-sharpening Chilled Shares & Coulter Blades
...NERS, HAYMAKERS, HORSE RAKES, STEAM ENGINES, THRASHING MACHINES, CORN MILLS, &c.,
...RUSHING AND GRINDING MILLS, CAKE BREAKERS, CHAFF CUTTERS, PULPERS; MOWERS, REAPERS AND BINDERS;
...TORS, CHURNS, BUTTER WORKERS, &c    TELEGRAMS—"COLLINONS, BEVERLEY."    NAT. TEL. 144.

## OPENING NIGHT, MONDAY, FEBRUARY 20TH.

**Under the Patronage and Presence of His Right Worshipful the Mayor (Councillor Sammon),**
AND OTHER MEMBERS OF THE CORPORATION.

# "IMPERATOR" CINEMATOGRAPH PICTURES.

### CORN EXCHANGE, BEVERLEY.

A HIGH CLASS PROGRAMME AT POPULAR PRICES  -  -  6d.  4d.  2d.

**TWICE NIGHTLY.**   7.   9.

Including The Opening of Parliament by King George V.: Bird Nesting on Flambro' Head, taken through the courtesy of the N.E.R. Kinsal Council Pathé Fréres, entitled "A Drama of 200 years ago": Comedy of how Jones tested his wife's courage; also, many other humorous and exciting pictures.    Early Doors 6.45 and 8.45.

If you wish to be interested, thrilled, and have a hearty laugh, don't miss these Pictures.

*The Playhouse opening night.*

# The Picture Playhouse,

## MARKET PLACE, BEVERLEY.

# PROGRAMMES.

### WEEK COMMENCING
### JUNE 1ST, 1914. ❊

**Early Doors Open - - - 6-20.**

**Two Houses Monday, Thursday, Saturday.**

**Continuous Tuesday, Wednesday, Friday.**

PROPRIETORS:

L. C. HOLDERNESS.                    E. F. SYMMONS.

Wright & Hoggard, Printers, Minster Press, Beverley.

*Programme for Whit Monday, 1st June, 1914.*

*Mock tank for the film, Battle of the Ancre, March 1917.*

ESTABLISHED
ALL OVER THE WORLD.

BRANCHES
BRITISH ISLES.

BIRMINGHAM,
303, Broad Street.
CARDIFF,
13. Charles Street.
GLASGOW,
80, Miller Street.
LEEDS,
1-8, Wellington Chambers.
LIVERPOOL,
34, Paradise St.
MANCHESTER,
15, Deansgate.
NEWCASTLE,
208, Westgate Road.
DUBLIN,
2, Lower Abbey Street.

HEAD OFFICES:
BRITISH ISLES,
84 & 103-109 WARDOUR St.
LONDON. W

TELEGRAMS,
Sales Dept.
PATHIREMA, OX.
Head Office.
PHONOFILM, OX.
TELEPHONES,
Sales Dept.
2842 REGENT,
3 LINES
Head Office,
2836 REGENT,
3 LINES

PATHÉ FRÈRES

CINEMA LIMITED.
REGISTERED OFFICE 21, BUCKLERSBURY, LONDON, E.C.
ASSOCIATED WITH
LA COMPAGNIE GÉNÉRALE DES ETABLISSEMENTS.
PATHÉ FRÈRES.
CAPITAL £1,200,000.
ALSO WITH
PATHÉ EXCHANGE, INC, N.Y.

IN REPLY PLEASE QUOTE
Ref
Dep

**Our bright rays of Joy & Laughter over your Programmes with Pathé SUNBEAMS**

Released every Monday
Send for Trial Copy.

Telephone
2856 REGENT.
(5 lines)

Telegrams:
"PHONOFILM," OX, LONDON.

*HEAD OFFICE—*

103-109, WARDOUR STREET,

LONDON, W. 1.

Aug. 30th, 1921.

Messrs. Debenham & Co.,
"Tropical House,"
Holgate Road,
York.

Dear Sirs,

<u>re FILM OF THE R-38</u>

        This is my first opportunity of writing
to thank you for your promptness and kindness in
helping us on this all-important event, and confirm
our wire congratulating you on your negative. The
Management of the Company are pleased to pass payment of £50. for this negative, and trust that on
all future occasions you will render us your best
services.

        I trust that the negative despatched to-day
to Mr. Symmons has reached him in time to enable him
to obtain the required pictures. I can assure you
that had I obtained Mr. Symmons telegram, I should
have seen that this negative was despatched at once,
as I am only too pleased to assist you in any way.

        Again thanking you for your kind attention
etc.,

        Your faithfully

*The tragedy of the R38. Letter from Pathe to Ernest Symmons.*

*Ernest Symmons on location at the Beverley Cottage Hospital, filming a Bonny Baby competition.*

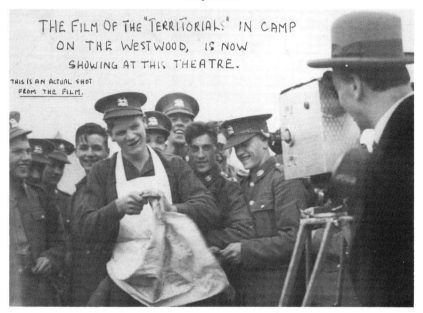

*Ernest Symmons filming the Territorials in camp on Beverley Westwood.*

## CHAPTER TWO

**The Arrival of Sound**

Although not widely know, some of the first experiments for recording sound on film go back as far as 1906!

A Frenchman, Eugene A. Lauste, after moving to England, had experimented in sound recording, and he later was to describe his apparatus 'as little more than a toy', but by 1910 he had recorded sound as a wide and variable area soundtrack on film alongside the picture. Unfortunately, with the coming of the First World War, his work ended without any commercial developments. It is a pity that no method could be found to amplify the signals generated by his sound projector; it was to be many years later before Lauste's system was fully developed. Although improved, his system is still in use today.

Around 1925-6 the Western Electric Sound film system had been demonstrated to Samuel L. Warner of Warner Brothers. This led to the Vitaphone Corporation being formed and was to provide the cinema-going public with their first sound films on the Vitaphone sound-on-disc system. For projection the film was threaded in the projector with a frame of film marked 'START' in the gate, and the pick-up needle was placed in the centre groove of the disc. Both the projector and turntable were driven by the same motor and started together when switched on, the two remaining in exact synchronisation throughout the reel. Even though they were sound-on-disc, the 16 inch records being synchronised with the projected image, frequent breakages added to the many problems of the system, which after a short time was to be discontinued in favour of optical sound-on-film.

The sound-on-disc method of producing 'talkies' became an immediate success, mainly due to Al Jolson in 'The Jazz Singer' (1927, Dir: Alan Crosland), but not all the successes have originated from across the Atlantic, for in 1929 right here in Britain our own Ernest Symmons produced what has been referred to as the first long out-door talkie produced in Yorkshire, described as a 'song film', 'Riverside Melodies' with popular songs of the period like 'You're the Cream in my Coffee'; 'You Were Meant for Me' and 'The Wedding of the Painted Doll'. The film was little more than a gentle musical interpretation of love's young dream on the river, but proved popular with audiences of the day. I have spoken to many people who saw 'Riverside Melodies' and found them to have fond memories of this film and its songs.

'Riverside Melodies' was made at Knaresborough for the Electrocord Company, the sound being of the disc system, this often posing problems if the disc became separated in transit from the film; (quite a common occurrence, I understand).

One reviewer of the day wrote of 'Riverside Melodies', 'A rather pleasing attraction for good class halls'. Another thought it was too long. Tragically, like so many films made by Ernest, there is no surviving record of this film.

Sound films, or 'Talkies' as they were more commonly known, were, without question, gaining popularity, although some doubted their success, believing the novelty would not last. They were soon proved wrong. In Europe and the United States 'Talkies' were the accepted norm by the early 30's. In the United Kingdom the race for the installation of sound reproducing equipment was fierce, especially as demand exceeded supply.

Here in Beverley, the coming of sound was to herald the first noted rivalry between the Picture Playhouse and the Marble Arch Cinema.

Ernest Symmons entered into a gentleman's agreement with Jos Butt, [4] Manager of the Marble Arch Cinema, that should their 'Talkies' equipment be available first, three months notice would be given to Ernest, thus enabling him to have a fair chance with a simultaneous sound opening.

Thankfully, Ernest had friends within the cinema trade, and one of them the Manager of the Tower Cinema in York, discovered that Western Electric sound apparatus was waiting in York station for installation at the Marble Arch.

After the initial shock of this news, Ernest immediately set about playing the opposition at their own game and planned to beat them.

The news threw the staff into a state of total chaos. The race was on. During the days of frantic installation the staff often worked until the early hours of the morning. Fortunately for Ernest his operators shared his enthusiasm.

The sound equipment Ernest installed was totally constructed by himself. This was a sound-on-disc system affording excellent quality. The first sound film to be tested was a trailer for the film 'Interference', Paramount's first full talking picture starring the late William Powell. On the screen appeared a large linen hoop, which split from the top to bottom with William Powell walking through and saying: 'Ladies and Gentlemen'. You can imagine the excitement of Ernest and staff at hearing those memorable words.

Well, the Playhouse did beat the Marble Arch, and the 'Beverley Guardian' dated February 22nd, 1930 advertised at the Picture Playhouse the first 'Talkie' picture 'The Home Towners' (1928 Dir: William McGann) for three days only from Monday, February 24th. This was the very first

[4] Jos Butt was the son of Edward Butt, a public licencee. Edward being one of the three partners who were originally responsible for the opening of the Marble Arch Cinema in 1916.

'talkie' picture to be seen and heard in Beverley and offered the cinema-goer nine acts of 'diverting dialogue'! For the remaining three days of that week the record-breaking success 'The Singing Fool' (1928 Dir: Lloyd Bacon) was screened.

A month later on March 22nd, 1930 the 'Beverley Guardian' announced the 'Grand Opening' on Monday, March 24th of the 'World Famous Western Electric Sound System at the Marble Arch Picture House'.

Although talkies had arrived at the Playhouse, I was very surprised to discover that silent films were to continue for many months. This was especially interesting as all the programmes screened at the Marble Arch were talkie or advertised as having 'synchronised sound', [5] while the Playhouse, one week, offered an all talkie programme, then the following week only half would be sound, or a silent programme for a full week but with a sound serial.

On silent nights the admission prices reverted to the pre-talkie prices, and usually included community singing. The 1930 Easter week film was 'Ramona' (1917, Dir: Donald Crisp). This was a full silent programme and there was no community singing. However, and almost as a consolation, there was to be a matinee on Good Friday if wet. Of course, the programme was not totally silent — the cinema still had musicians.

At the end of April I came across an advertisement for the showing of the last silent film made by Norma Talmadge, 'The Woman Disputed' (1928, Dirs: Henry King/Sam Taylor). This would, I thought, surely be the last silent film I could find. The following week the long-awaited film, 'Interference' (1929, Dirs: Lothar Mendes/Roy Pomeroy) arrived just over three months after the first talkie trailer had been demonstrated.

May 26th brought 'The Desert Song' (1929, Dir: Roy Delruth) with sound, but the following week it was back to silents for three days. This mixture of sound and silent films continued right until July 1930, after when all programmes had sound.

This final change to sound films arrived, I believe, when the sound-on-disc was superseded by the sound-on-film system thus eliminating the problem of lost and broken discs.

The 'Talkies' had arrived for good at the Playhouse, and as more films became available with sound, so the press advertisements announced, '100% dialogue', 'All talkie', 'All talking, singing and dancing', with 'prices for talking pictures 6d, 9d and 1/3, reserved 1/6, tax including'.

[5] I am told by Mrs. Symmons that the most likely reason for the Marble Arch screening so many films with sound compared to the Playhouse is thought to be due to their installation of the Western Electric sound system and the fact that the Marble Arch was one of a small circuit cinema chain with more sound products available to them. The independent Playhouse used the sound-on-disc system at first, and there was a smaller choice of product in this format. There was, however, a vast amount of silent material unseen when talkies arrived which, of course, the distributors still wanted to find outlets for. Obviously, the Playhouse was one such outlet.

Beverley people were also reminded 'that the Picture Playhouse was the first permanent house of entertainment in Beverley to show *Silent Pictures;* also in spite of competition the *First 'Talkie' Picture* was heard in this Hall, reproduced by a *British* installation of Original Design'. It was a large claim, but it was all true.

Even with sound films, on one occasion the audience was asked, 'Can You Lip Read?' Had talkies failed as critics predicted? No. This was one of Ernest's competitions with £5 offered in prizes if you could read the lip movement of one of the actors. The announcement in the 'Beverley Guardian' carried one important request to participants in this quiz — to bring a lead pencil with them!

Another competition was advertised as 'A New Film Judging Competition', readers of the 'Beverley Guardian' being invited to forecast the popularity in entertainment value from a list of '12 Super Films'; first prize £10 and runner-up prizes of season tickets.

For winners in the 1931 'Xmas Prize Competition' there was no cash or free tickets but 'A lady's Permanent Wave as 1st; 2nd — English turkey and 3rd — box of 100 cigarettes', and the 'Big Christmastide Attractions' at the Playhouse were no less than six changes of programme in six days including five matinees one each on Christmas Day and Boxing Day with a special children's morning performance.

One week in early 1932, a popular local newsreel showed film of 'Local Ladies playing Football'. In contrast, later the same week, a short musical interlude was presented by Miss Kostrovitzki's Quintet. Throughout the same year I found many references to other musical presentations at the cinema. This surprised me for I thought with the popularity of sound it would have been easier to reproduce gramophone records, thus disposing with those many temperamental musicians. But this was not to be the case, for July 1932 brought Syd Braithwaite and his Merry Boys to entertain with Melody and Jazz twice nightly on Wednesdays and Saturdays, and later the same month The New Orchestra under the direction of H. Francis Fawcett played the latest popular numbers on Wednesday and Saturday nights, and in August The New Orchestra again played while Mr. Louis Gould, 'The Monarch of Melody', entertained.

Local and topical films were still to attract audiences to the Playhouse during 1933, two of them being 'The Saga of Hunmanby' and 'The Wonderful Catholic Procession', both films being made by Ernest, the latter was recommended as having 'special appeal' to all who took part.

1933, I believe, was a milestone year in the Playhouse history. This was the year of Beverley's First Carnival Queen Competition, and the beginning of what was to become a very popular and annual event for many years to be captured on film, with crownings and presentations of prizes taking place at the Playhouse.

During the same year, Ernest was approached by representatives of the

31

Hesslewood Orphanage. His photographic talents were desperately needed to help them raise funds for the re-building and upgrading of the Orphanage. I understand a film was 'specially' made to show the appalling conditions of the place. Its subsequent screenings had the desired effect of enrolling public support and funds to finance the redevelopment of the property. However, not all contributions came as a result of the film's exhibition. A 'Grand Concert' was held at the Playhouse with admission by programme, and proceeds supporting this worthy cause.

The very hot summer of 1934 brought announcements from both the Marble Arch and the Picture Playhouse, stating that during the hot weather and until further notice there would be only one show nightly, except Thursdays and Saturdays. Other items of interest in the same year were a fancy dress contest at the Marble Arch, while the Playhouse hosted the Carnival Queen Competition, now with a first prize of £25, an event which I'm sure must have been filmed for Ernest's local newsreel (although I can find no record).

The popularity of local newsreels produced by Ernest continued and was very much in evidence, this being apparent by numerous favourable press reports in 1935, and as the Playhouse claimed to be 'The only Theatre in the Country which runs its own News Reel' this legend and title was invariably greeted by a round of applause, and with weekly changes on Thursday afternoons, 'The Playhouse News' was very much up to date, all events 'Filmed and Edited by E. F. Symmons, Beverley'.

Some of the 'newsy' items presented in 'The Playhouse News' were 'Sunday School assembling and leaving the Market for Wesley Chapel'; 'Coronation of Miss Beverley'; 'Old English Fayre'; 'Babies Competition'; 'A Special film of Troops going to the Minster'; 'Cricket Season Ends — Football Season Starts'; 'Ladies Golf Tournament'; 'Wedding of Miss Joan Whitehead and Mr. F. Johnson'. As you will see from these titles the subjects were varied and would definitely attract audiences to the cinema.

During 1935, Ernest fought hard against duplicated films. The problem was caused by excessive duty being levied on imported developed negatives from America, and often prohibitive costs of bringing distribution copies across the Atlantic, so the outcome was that a duplicate negative (often of dubious quality) was brought into the country, and from this other negatives were made and eventually the distribution positives.

Of course, the films shown at the trade show were of an impeccable quality being struck from the master negative, but when the films reached the provinces their quality was usually appalling, this being a fair indication that they had been 'duped'. In fact claims were made that 90% of the films around during this problem period were 'duped' copies. [6]

[6] I feel the reader may understand the 'duped' film problem slightly better if I liken it to the copying of videos. If all are made from the quality master — no problems, but start copying copies of copies, as happens with video piracy, and the quality continues to deteriorate. Visualise the small 35mm frame of film, just imagine the number of times it has to be magnified to fill the large cinema screens of the day, any defects will also be magnified, not only in picture but also sound.

Mention must be made that Ernest once had ideas for a new Super Cinema in the town. Plans had been prepared for a combined cinema with dance hall above, and the development was planned for a piece of land in Lord Robert's Road, which attracted favourable discussions with the Town Clerk, Mr. John Dennett.

I understand these plans were studied in detail by Messrs. Watts and Tarran, who were to be the two men responsible for the development and conversion of The Assembly Rooms, to what was to become the Regal Cinema. (The Assembly Rooms, if you recall from my earlier notes, had been the building in which cinematograph shows had been held in 1897).

The Regal development went ahead at great speed, the foundation stone being laid on August 3rd, 1935, by the Mayor, Councillor W. E. Brumfield. Ernest was repeatedly begged to join this venture, but declined each time; he was soon thankful he had done so when the property changed hands.

I feel that the development and construction of the Regal Cinema may have been instrumental in the transformations taking place at the Playhouse. A new flexible glass screen, one of the best available, was installed and this gave an almost stereoscopic effect to the projected image at the Playhouse, especially with coloured pictures.

The screen, however, was not the only improvement in 1935, the theatre had been beautifully decorated by Mr. F. Fairfield. The ceilings and beams were painted in 'artistic shades' and presented a very impressive effect when illuminated by the green ceiling lights. The work was done so well that at no time were the audiences in any way inconvenienced.

New and more comfortable seats of the very latest design were fitted, measuring twenty inches across the back instead of the usual eighteen, the backs were deep and the seat springing afforded the greatest possible comfort, not forgetting the 'pneumatic' arm rests!

The thick and luxurious Imperial Axminster carpets had been supplied by Messrs. Gresswell & Sons and the felting was undertaken by Messrs. E. Elwell & Son, both of Beverley.

Golden coloured sun-ray curtains made from about six hundred yards of material, along with velvet curtains and pelmets were supplied by Messrs. M. Reynolds. Wherever possible, the work had been entrusted to local tradespeople who had all satisfactorily fulfilled their contracts.

New lighting effects were very pleasing, giving an overall feeling of sunshine and warmth. Other improvements included 'new air cleaning apparatus' and a number of small silent electric fans placed at the rear of the theatre.

The cinema looked magnificent, and as one cinemagoer wrote in his letter to 'The Announcer' the Playhouse 'compared favourably with some of the London suburban theatres, so justly famed for their artistic interior decorations' — a compliment indeed.

In late August, while fitting new cables in the roof of St. Mary's Church, electricians discovered signs that the dreaded and devastating Death Watch

Beetle was at work. A full and detailed examination was to reveal that many parts of the Church roof were in a precarious position. The four-hundred year old beams had almost been eaten away, and immediate rectification was needed to make the structure safe. The estimated cost was at least £10,000.

You may be wondering what all this has to do with Ernest and the Playhouse? Well, Ernest volunteered his services to produce a film depicting the damage caused by the Beetle, and progress reports of reconstruction.

The film was called 'The Villain in the Wood' and was screened at the Playhouse with the Rev. T. H. Tardrew, L.L.B., [7] giving a commentary at each performance explaining the damage done by the Beetle.

A collection was made after each house, and at the end of the week the patrons had contributed £41-10s-6d (£41.52½) to the restoration fund.

The film received an excellent press along with the highest praises and thanks from Rev. Tardrew and church authorities.

Something I found very interesting in the production notes for the film may have been a clue to an enquiry made in the early sixties by a firm specialising in pest eradication. The notes read as follows: 'For the filming of the picture, special cinematograph lamps were installed in the roof of the Church and interesting effects were observed on the insects reaction to them, the strong actinic light killing them almost at once'.

I could not help but wonder if, by accident, Ernest had stumbled upon an easy or inexpensive way of eradicating these villains?! (I have contacted various firms of pest eradicators in an attempt to research this enquiry, but to no avail).

Saturday, November 7th, 1935, was the date on which the Regal opened in Beverley, and it was to offer cinemagoers the very latest in comfort and luxury. Seating in the cinema, including balcony, was for approximately 1,000. This was the ultimate in entertainment, for not only did the building incorporate the cinema, but also a large ballroom with sprung maple floor above the cinema, with roof gardens for the summer months.

The building was practically gutted and the main entrance was completely re-built, and rounded off with swing doors leading to an 'oval vestibule' complete with payboxes. Inside the foyer, patrons could relax and wait in comfortable chairs and setees before entering the super, air-conditioned theatre, which also had facilities for partially deaf people enabling them, with the aid of 'special earphones', to hear 'the whole of the words and music of the films'.

The Regal opened with a Grand Ceremony. All the important people were there, including The Mayor (Councillor W. E. Brumfield), Ernest Symmons and quite a few other local dignitaries. A fanfare was presented

[7] The Reverand Thomas Hedley Tardrew, L.L.B., was vicar of St. Mary's Church, Beverley, between 1933 and 1954 and became Canon and Precentor of York in 1944.

by Trumpeters of the 15th and 16th Lancers. Hodgson's Silver Band of Beverley gave a musical programme with Miss Marjorie Jones as soloist. The opening film was Robert Donat in 'The 39 Steps' (1935, Dir: Alfred Hitchcock).

I cannot help but wonder just what Ernest must have felt on the two occasions competition loomed, with the opening of the Marble Arch and then the Regal. No doubt he must have frequently thought that in no way could his little cinema match the luxury or comfort afforded by the 'big boys'.

I feel this competition must have caused some tremendous worries for Ernest and staff, probably more so with the property only being leased, and with what I discovered was an often and real threat, that of a proposed extension of the Public Baths through into the cinema. How could anyone comfortably compete never knowing for how long you would be secure?

As time was to prove, the Playhouse did survive and compete with the 'big boys' and outlived them to prove it. I don't think survival would have been possible had it not been for Ernest's involvement with local news items. The 'Beverley Guardian' wrote that 'The Picture Playhouse News is definitely recording the history of this old town', and went on to say that film had already been taken of the shipyard and that further additions are to be made. Plans were also in hand to film Hodgson's Tannery, The Glue Works and the Gordon Armstrong Works.

In 1936 the 'Playhouse News' continued to present items like 'The One Armed Cyclist' attempting to break the world record and being welcomed in Beverley; 'Laying of the Foundation Stone for the New Grammar School'; 'Founders' Day Parade'; 'Puppy Judging at Rise Park', and musical interludes were not overlooked, with the Special Engagement of Ron Wakelin and his Continental Accordion Band, which proved to be a great attraction.

As the year progressed a 'You And Your Dog' competition was held, and the New Grammer School was opened by Viscount Halifax K.C.T.

'Alone With The Monster!' quoted 'Universal Weekly' as a heading to an article regarding a publicity stunt of Ernest's. Curious? Allow me to explain. This was the challenge from Ernest, offering a £2 reward to any young woman with sufficient pluck to sit through a midnight screening of 'The Bride of Frankenstein'. (1935, Dir: James Whale). So far this probably doesn't seem too scary, but wait. The whole theatre was to be in total darkness during the film's screening. However, it seems that the fair sex of Beverley in 1936 were a very brave lot, for over a hundred letters were received from ladies prepared to brave this ordeal. One wrote: 'Dear Sir; If you can find me a bigger monster, with worse cravings than the one I have been living with for the past thirteen years, I am prepared to meet him any time, any place!'

The stunt was a huge success, and sucured excellent press coverage, giving the film a great deal of valuable publicity.

March 1937 brought many of the town's industries to the screen. The 'News' toured the industries which had been visited by His Worship the Mayor. These included The Ropery, Armstrongs, The Brass Works and Waggon Works. Other items included, George Formby at a local stable, school children celebrating the Coronation in The Market Place, and film of the children's Coronation tea at Sparkmill Terrace.

The B.B.C. Broadcast of the actual Coronation Day ceremony started at 10.30 a.m. on May 1st, and if you were lucky enough to have an invitation you could hear the ceremony 're-diffused' at the Playhouse, and on the same day at the second house you had the opportunity of seeing a short film of the Coronation 'brought by aeroplane by H. L. Brook (the Famous air pilot)'.

Up to this point I have referred only to the odd short lengths of film made by Ernest that have survived the years. 1937 brought to the screen 'Beverley Through The Ages', which I would term as one of Ernest's best surviving films, showing his expertise as producer, director, camera operator and editor. 'Beverley Through the Ages' is a photographic record of a Pageant Procession depicting historical events, many in Beverley and district, from the times of the 'Early Britons' to 1937. Judging by the size of the procession it was quite an event. I have been told that over 2000 colourful costumes were used for the occasion, although regretfully the film was only made in monochrome.

A particular episode I always find amusing is the one dealing with sanctuary in the town with 'dramatic' acting and a 'double take' of a fugitive on the run. It looks as though it should have been edited out at some time; however, left in it seldom fails to raise a laugh. The Carnival Queens are not overlooked in this production, for as I have mentioned before, these became annual events. 1937 was no exception, for this one shows no less than six 'Miss Beverleys' representing sister towns throughout the world. The conclusion of this 'epic' lasting just over twenty minutes, is a charming romantic drama set in the early days of the Victorian era, filmed at Bishop Burton. It's the story of elopement and eventual marriage at the Blacksmith's Shop. I think this episode beautifully concludes 'Beverley Through The Ages'. For many years I understand the film was narrated 'live' by Ernest, until he decided to tape a narrative to accompany the film. I found from experience the sound and visuals never fail to fascinate and amuse an audience, especially those who spot themselves.

I am fortunate in having my own copy of this film, so have had the opportunity to study it. Apart from my own, a 35mm copy has been deposited in The National Film Archive for permanent preservation, along with taped narration by Ernest Symmons himself.

During the latter part of a year, in which local industry had featured so much on the news scene, came the grand tour of the Tannery. However, this was not like the earlier factory visits; it was 'Beverley's First Local Sound Film' entitled, 'The Romance of Leather'. I feel sure readers who were familiar with the Tannery and its smells would question the word 'Romance' in the title.

The Tannery was that of Richard Hodgson & Sons Ltd., which, at the time, was one of the major industries in the town. Fortunately at the time of writing a copy of the film still survives. On the whole it's an interesting film, and I especially like the opening shots of the 'leather on the hoof' standing with the Westwood as a back-drop. Sadly, most of Beverley's industries, including the tannery, covered by the 'News' are no longer in existence and this makes the film of immense value to historians both of film and of industry.

1937 brought to the screen a Diamond Wedding, the opening of Armstrong Patents' new factory, and scenes of the Beverley and East Riding Laundry (both industries have since closed). Also featured were the weddings of Dora Cherry to Charles Sheppard, Linda Fisher to Alwyn Middleton, Stephen Elder to Joyce Bloomfield and Joyce Stamford to James Dean, and probably the most outstanding attraction of the year was not an Ernest Symmons production, but Walt Disney's, 'Snow White and the Seven Dwarfs' (1937). Due to the high cost of this production and special conditions imposed, it was not possible to admit children at reduced rates for evening performances. However, with daily matinees and a Saturday morning show they were well catered for. With tea-time and evening performances, 'Snow White' was screened twenty times in the week. (Forty-five years later, in December 1983, 'Snow White' was successfully screened again; and even with an extra show some people were turned away).

# CHAPTER THREE

## The Sound of Sirens

With the outbreak of the Second World War, the Playhouse was to take on a new role in its continuing service to the community, not just as a cinema — but as a church, proving that blackout restrictions need not stop services during the winter months, when any attempt to blackout church windows would have been impossible.

Rev. T. H. Tardrew, vicar of St. Mary's Church once again found a friend in Ernest, who placed the Playhouse at his disposal for Sunday evening services.

Conforming with regulations the congregation all carried their gas masks, and for a quarter of an hour before the service, records of sacred tunes were played over the cinema's loud speakers. The organist from St. Mary's played the piano for hymns and psalms, while the choir sang from the front row of the stalls. Within weeks the new venue and comfort had proved so successful that even with chairs in the aisles and people occupying all the balcony steps, many were turned away.

These services were to continue throughout the winter months of the war, and I have been told by many people who attended how wonderful they were, and they were appreciated even more with the addition of the hymn words projected onto the screen.

The war was to affect the lives of practically everyone in the country, but during the dark years people did find the cinema afforded a great escape from their daily problems and fears, and at the same time brought home to them through newsreels the work our Armed Forces were doing abroad.

At the Playhouse every effort was made to boost morale and generally keep spirits high. Competitions were held for the members of the audience to enter. One described as a 'Go as you please Competition' was for members of H. M. Forces in uniform only, with a first prize of £2. On the occasion of a Sunday night concert, many military personnel provided 'excellent entertainment', while during the second part of the programme Rev. Tardrew acted as compere in a novelty number entitled, 'I want to be an actor'.

I have heard stories of how Ernest opened up the Playhouse to the many troops stationed in the surrounding area, and how the wounded were brought into the cinema in wheelchairs and on stretchers. Fortunately, standing room was available for quite a number of patrons — and I have heard of 'dozens' of wheelchairs etc., being parked within the area — at no charge; on the contrary, Ernest rewarded these soldiers in kind with liberal gifts of cigarettes, tobacco and sweets. This was confirmed when one day I chatted with an old soldier who, while passing through Beverley on holiday, wanted to see the cinema where he had had such happy times during the war. This man confirmed, without prompting, the generosity bestowed upon him and his colleagues by the manager.

During the night of May 7th, 1941 the city of Hull was severely bombed. Four-hundred people were killed and eight-hundred injured. 3,000 homes were completely wrecked and 50,000 damaged. Ironically this is the material for making good news coverage, as was the Royal visit to Hull on August 6th, when King George VI and Queen Elizabeth visited the blitzed areas.

'Playhouse News' was to become rather special, as it was believed to be the first film of a blitzed city, with the exception of London, that showed the extensive damage done by the Lufftwaffe, and after viewing, it was released by the censor for public exhibition in this country.

After a special preview of this film at the Dorchester Cinema, Hull, Viscount Halifax thought that this excellent production was just the sort of film the Americans would wish to see, and would be delighted to take a copy back to America which he would personally present to President Roosevelt, thus ensuring its incorporation in the American Newsreels.

Thanks to the generosity of the Sheriff of Hull, numerous copies of the film were made and distributed to many parts of the world, with the hope that those who saw the film would contribute to the Hull Air Raid Distress Fund.

June 14th, 1941 saw the start of Beverley's 'War Weapons Week'. Ernest was elected as Honorary Secretary to the Publicity Committee and as well as his official duties during this period he also managed to film many of the events. Two surviving films I have seen show dancing at Norwood cricket ground and Aircraft in the Market Place, (one of these being a damaged Messerschmitt). At the end of the week it was thanks all round. A grand total of £282,378 had been raised.

Around this time, Ernest produced a short six-minute film entitled, 'How to deal with Incendiary Bombs'. Its content being as the title describes, the film was favourably received throughout the area, and was commended by the fire authorities.

Another short but surviving Playhouse News is the 'Warship Week' parade of 1942. 'Warship Week' was an attempt to persuade people to invest their money in War Savings Certificates and Government Bonds. Here in Beverley, as the film shows, a large mock-up of a warship was made and was seen in Saturday and Wednesday Markets as a prop for the parade. The event was filmed during early March, and judging by the chilled looks of the participants, the weather must have been very cold. During

'Warship Week' a midnight matinee of 'Professor Mamlock' (1938, Dir: Adolf Minken/Herbert Rappopart) was held. The entire proceeds were donated to the cause.

A slightly happier occasion, worthy of mention in those days of gloom, was the invitation extended to children of prisoners of war, and their next of kin, to a special matinee at the Playhouse to see the Walt Disney film 'Dumbo' (1941, Dir: Ben Sharpsteen), organised by a local J. P. assisted by the Citizen's Advice Bureau and the Rotary Club. After the matinee the children were treated to tea at the Rambla Cafe.

When, in 1943, the 'Epic of British Military Achievement', 'Desert Victory' (1943, Dir: Roy Boulting) was exhibited, five screenings daily were advertised with special performances during the mornings for H. M. Forces only. During the week over 3,000 Forces members were guests of Ernest and, for the record, a short film was made on the Monday morning of the soldiers entering and leaving the Cinema. This was shown a week later, and no doubt attracted quite a bit of extra business.

A programme with a difference was one sponsored by the Ministry of Information in connection with the Merchant Navy Effort. Between the films Mr. Colin Armitage talked of his experiences as a survivor spending fifty days on a raft, after his ship was torpedoed in the Mid-Atlantic.

For the third time since the outbreak of war the area received a Royal visitor, the second time for Beverley, but a first for the Playhouse. H.R.H. The Princess Royal, called during her visit to W.V.S. centres in the area. This was September 18th, 1944, and was the first time Royalty had visited a cinema in this district. A very impressive Guard of Honour by smart young hospital helps stood to attention at the entrance to the cinema, Her Royal Highness acknowledging them with a smile.

The Princess Royal had visited the town in 1941, an event, of course, filmed by Ernest, and shown to her now. He delivered the running commentary himself. However, the film the Princess had really come to see was that which Ernest had captured of the W.V.S. Hospital Helps and the wonderful work these youngsters did to help patients in the emergency hospital. A party of these patients was invited to be part of this special occasion. It's also worth noting that according to the 'Beverley Guardian' Her Royal Highness expressed her pleasure and approval of the films presented.

Besides the activities of war, there was still great concern for those killed and injured on the roads and much publicity was given to road safety. The Beverley branch of the Royal Society for the Prevention of Accidents joined forces with Ernest to produce a film dealing with road safety entitled simply 'Safety First'. This film, I believe, may have been a 'pilot' for the more ambitious film 'The Man With The Notebook', my belief being based purely on the subject matter.

1945 was the year of 'The Man With The Notebook'. This was the first 'talkie' safety film to be made outside of London, and was regarded by Road

Safety Authorities as one of the best films dealing with this subject. The Blackburn Aircraft Company of Brough was persuaded to contribute £500 towards the cost of producing 'The Man With The Notebook'. In fact, this film had an incredibly low production cost when compared to other contemporary films dealing with the same subject. The 35mm copy was shown in every commercial cinema in the East and West Ridings of Yorkshire, to a total audience of 297,555. The 16mm copy was shown to people in 120 villages and towns in the East Riding and 44 copies were sold throughout the country, including a copy each for Accra and Ceylon. At the time of release it was well accepted, but today I find it just a little too melancholy even for the seriousness of the subject. This is, I feel, mainly due to the commentary being spoken rather monotonously by the Chief Constable of the East Riding. I just wish there had been more life in his voice.

The film is, in my view, flawless with the exception of a slight synchronisation problem, which had been discussed at great length with the Imperial Sound Studios. The film is presented in two principal episodes; 'The Case of the Open Gate' and 'The Case of Richard Shaw'. In both cases we are allowed time to interest ourselves in the characters, which is particularly effective when a near accident or tragedy occurs practically forcing us to reflect that these could have been our own relatives. In the 'Open Gate' episode the little girl was played by Jennifer Welland, and in the 'Richard Shaw' sequence Shaw was played by Fred Leonard, a well known Hull character actor. It is interesting to note that the Beverley pub, the Rose and Crown played host studio to Richard Shaw's domino game, and although a few changes have taken place with modernisation of the Rose and Crown, it is still recognisable today.

'The Man With The Notebook' allows a peep at some of Beverley town past, including Norwood, the old Globe Inn and Ladygate. These are the scenes I never tire of seeing, although no copy is known to exist for public access I am thankful I have my own.

A novel children's show was organised in connection with the book and paper salvage drive. Admission to the special film show was free, but to gain entrance, children had to bring books or magazines and the more books they brought the better the seat they got.

A large queue of excited children waited outside the cinema for a considerable time, so many that they almost filled it to capacity. As a result of the show nearly a ton of paper was collected for allocation to either the forces or munitions.

As the war ends, mention must be made of the 'Hull Victory Celebrations' film. This was, as the title implies, a record of the victory celebrations, skillfully photographed, but enhanced with the excellent voice of the famous Alvar Lidell who was paid ten guineas for his services. [8]

[8] Alvar Lidell was born in London, the son of a Swedish family. He joined the B.B.C. in Birmingham in 1932, and succeeded Stuart Hubbard as the senior announcer on London's national radio in 1933. Although radio announcers of the day remained anonymous, Lidell always announced, 'Here is the news, my name is Alvar Lidell', which obviously made him one of the best known personalities on radio. Lidell retired from broadcasting in 1969, and died on January 7th, 1981 in Northwood, Middlesex.

# CHAPTER FOUR

## A Time for change and innovation

An early Playhouse Newsreel of 1947 contained a memorable and historical event. It was film of the ceremony on January 16th of the presentation of the Freedom of the Borough to Councillor and Mrs. Arthur Watts. Scenes also included the commemoration dinner in the Regal cafe and dance in the Regal ballroom.

Shortly afterwards, the Playhouse was loaned back to the Beverley Corporation, and in place of the usual Thursday matinee, the Mayor, Alderman H. S. Nicholson, presented the Freedom of the Borough to two of its worthy citizens, Squadron Leader A. V. Duffill, D.F.C., and C.S.M. (Mrs.) Purvis, A.T.S. This event was, of course, filmed for the News and screened a week later.

Around the same time the Playhouse was showing a very large number of British films. Did the public want British films? The Management wanted to know and offered several prizes for the best postcard stating, in not more than 100 words (!), which pictures patrons had enjoyed the most, and the type of film they wanted for the future; for some it wasn't a case of what was showing, but when it would be shown; for in a survey carried out amongst soldiers in the area, 99 out of every 100 favoured Sunday cinema. This may have prompted the owners of the Regal and management of the Marble Arch Cinema to submit a petition signed by 195 people requesting the Town Council take necessary steps under the 1932 Entertainment Act to enable cinemas in Beverley to open on Sundays for film shows. However, the Council did not approve as only four members favoured the public vote, and after all, as one Councillor commented, even those people working all week had all day Saturday to visit the pictures.

Ernest was not keen on this Sunday opening; He felt Sundays meant additional labour and he wasn't prepared to ask his staff to work more hours each week.

Judging by letters sent to the press, Beverley cinemagoers were not too pleased at the decision against Sunday opening. The alternative was to pay 1/1d (5½p) bus fare, or twice that for the train, and then often having to queue for up to an hour, only to find it necessary to leave ten minutes before the end of the film to catch the last service home. Suggestions came from the public to open all three cinemas, and if the people didn't want them they would close. The cry went out to let the people choose. After all, they could play golf, cricket, tennis, have concerts, motor and drink on Sundays, so why could they not have pictures?

Like Ernest, the Playhouse staff were not in favour of opening either, and as it was to be quite a few years before the decision was reversed, they were happy continuing with their free Sundays.

Monday, December 15th brought an exclusive to the Playhouse with 'The Royal Wedding' (HRH The Princess Elizabeth to Philip Mountbatten) film. This was 'the official and only Technicolor film' of the occasion, and so popular was the film that extra shows had to be put on including two morning performances and a midnight matinee.

In the same week the feature film was 'Holiday Camp' (1947). This was the first film directed by Beverley born Ken Annakin, [9] and an additional bonus was that the film contained scenes of thousands of campers taken near Filey. This was 'a picture to appeal to all Beverlonians'.

I mentioned earlier in this chapter the problems that cinemagoing patrons from Beverley had when visiting cinemas in Hull, mainly having to leave before the end. Cinemagoers visiting Beverley from the surrounding villages were much luckier, for the bus company decided to arrange the last buses from Beverley to coincide with the cinemas turning out. It was nice to know you could catch the last kiss without missing the last bus.

At the time of publication I can find no record of any films being made by Ernest during the years 1949 to 1952. You may be interested to know that in 1948 Ernest presented to Beverley Corporation the collection of films he had made of events in the town and district over a period of twenty-five years.

The suggested safe accommodation for the films was the Strong Room at the Municipal Offices. This met with the full approval of Ernest and the County Chief Fire Officer.

Upon receipt of this gift the Mayor acknowledged Ernest's great interest in the social welfare of the town that had on many occasions prompted him to capture these events on film at great trouble and expense. It was felt these valuable and unique films may in years to come be as equally valuable as the Charter collection.

1950 brought 'Britain's Greatest Film' to the Playhouse. This was 'Hamlet', (1948, Dir: Laurence Olivier) winner of 38 awards including Best Picture, and with morning performanes for schools, pupils welcomed this break from the usual lessons. I know I always did whenever our school went to the pictures.

The film 'Hamlet' was used as a yardstick indicator in the battle of taxation on British films. For example, if you had paid 3/- (15p) for your

[9] Ken Annakin was born in 1914, and after a varied career outside of the film industry he joined Verity films. Invalided out of the RAF in 1942, Ken Annakin's first film was as co-director on the 1943 documentary 'London'. Recent films include 'The Call of the Wild' (1972) and 'Pirate' (1982).

seat to see 'Hamlet' you were putting 1/9 (9½p) into the pocket of the film exhibitor and 1/3 (6p) into the till of the Chancellor of the Exchequer.

However, had you paid the same amount to see Sir Laurence in the stage production of the play, the Chancellor would have been content with a rake-off of 4d (1½p) while the theatre owner would have been allowed to pocket the remaining 2/8 (14p). Thus the film exhibitor would be 11d (5p) poorer than the theatre owner on every 3/- (15p) paid. Could this possibly have been due to the theatre owners having to pay live actors?

The Chancellor of the Exchequer's desperate need to increase revenue to meet his massive post-war defence programme may have received a degree of sympathy in some circles, but the cinema exhibitor would be hit hard by the new taxation, forcing some into bankruptcy, and causing existing financial problems to multiply for others.

The new safety film stock was costing more, and since 1939 the cost of seating materials had gone up 430%, projector costs, 300%, and wages had doubled.

No doubt cinema owners throughout the country would appeal against the high taxes as did the mangers from Beverley's three cinemas. Their cries were in vain, because the taxation was to continue for many years to come.

During these times of high taxation, it was a pleasure to find that Ernest's generosity to his patrons was unaffected, for I came across a letter of thanks to Ernest from members of the Beverley Red Cross Old People's Club in the 'Beverley Guardian'. It appears that each Monday and Thursday afternoon members of this club had the pleasure of free admissions to the cinema. The club's organiser went on to express her thanks for the 'great joy' given by this anticipation of weekly happiness, and warmly recorded the gratitude of all who so regularly attended.

During March 1953, the manager of the Regal Cinema announced through the 'Beverley Guardian' that a three-dimensional film called 'Metroscopix' (1953) would be screened at his cinema. He went on to explain that the film would last for 20 minutes. Viewers would be supplied with polarised glasses free of charge.

The publicity for the film stated that the 3D effect would be most impressive. The viewer would apparantly see a girl swinging over the auditorium. The audience would also share a breathless ride on a Big Dipper and feel in the middle of the action. It was also claimed that the Beverley Regal was one of the first cinemas in the north of England to be chosen for the showing of 3D films. However, this claim was soon contested.

Ernest replied by stating respectfully, but most emphatically, that stereoscopic moving films had been shown at the Playhouse some 27 years earlier in 1925, and since that year 3D films had been shown over a period of several months.

These films were supposed to be short-length subjects, with free glasses being provided enabling the spectator to view them properly. However, their entertainment value was not great enough to warrant the Metro-Goldwyn-Mayer company to continue production of them.

The claim made by Ernest that he was first in town with 3D was substantiated by another reader who also remembered this novelty, especially as he battled with the usherette to retain his glasses.

The Regal manager replied by saying that most of the major American film companies were concentrating on the production of 3D films, while here in Britain men with foresight in the industry were making plans for equipping many of their cinemas to show 3D films. He went on to say that a crystal ball was not needed to see that in the not too distant future two dimensional films would be a thing of the past — mainly destined for television and not the cinema screen. He also added, the emphasis was now on the future and not on past achievements.

Well, history has provided the answer; 3D was not a great success, and even though it is enjoying a revival in the 80's I feel this too will be very short lived.

The Coronation of Her Majesty, Queen Elizabeth II was only a matter of months away, and as the newsreel coverage of this event was of great importance, the major news companies were wasting no time in promoting their forthcoming attractions. Word was brought to Ernest's ear that the Regal would be showing the Pathé version of the Coronation, 'Elizabeth is Queen' on June 15th. The Rank coverage destined for the Playhouse was 'A Queen is Crowned'. However, this would not be available for screening until June 22nd. Unfortunately, there was no possible way the release could be brought forward to correspond with the Regal opening. The Rank Organisation had agreed, in an effort to help, to share the additional publicity costs with Ernest, whatever they were, with no limit.

As you will have already realised, Ernest was not a man to just let things pass him by. He came forth with the startling idea to launch, in early April, a competition with a guarantee of attracting the widest possible interest and appeal in Beverley and district. This was to be the Great Coronation Year Baby Competition, run jointly between the Playhouse and 'Beverley Guardian'. So successful was this competition that I counted no less than 10 weeks of good press coverage reporting on the various stages of the event throughout its duration.

To enter, all you had to do was submit a recent photograph of a child aged between fifteen months to four years inclusive, twins counting as one child! A committee would select fourteen children who would then go forward to be filmed for final judging.

The response was incredible, with well over 500 photographs being received, and to quote the 'Beverley Guardian' 'these photographs clearly prove that children of the present generation are healthy, well-formed and most attractive'. A panel of judges headed by Mr. Fred Elwell R. A., had the difficult task of selecting the fourteen finalists who would go on to be filmed, and there was an added bonus here, in that the lucky babies would be given a copy of their film to keep.

Film taken of the finalists would be shown to coincide with the Coronation film 'A Queen is Crowned' on June 22nd. During that week members of the audience would be asked to vote for which child they liked best — not the best actor or actress or the most beautiful, but simply the child that appealed most to them.

You didn't turn your nose up at the prizes either, all of which were donated by local traders. D. & F. Electrical Stores had donated a television set as a first prize; others included a cycle for man or woman ( H. E. Akrill ), a Minton China tea service ( Drewry's ), a modern folding camera ( Selles Chemist ), a canteen of cutlery ( M. Heaps & Son ), a pressure cooker ( Briggs & Powell ), a cloth coat for a little boy or girl ( Miss Tiplady ) and many others.

The venues for filming the children were carefully selected. The playground at Butlin's Holiday Camp, Filey, Mr. Elwell's garden and the studios of Mr. S. Stephenson of the Rambla Garage were all kindly placed at the organiser's disposal.

As the competition gained momentum the original fourteen children to be filmed increased to twenty, and, as will be appreciated, this incurred great expense and above all patience.

On Monday morning, June 22nd, 1953, the Mayor and Mayoress ( Councillor and Mrs. P. Dennis Dunn ), along with many members of the Corporation and their wives, magistrates and Borough officials, attended a special performance of 'A Queen is Crowned' along with film of the twenty Beverley babies, and an invitation was extended to all the distinguished visitors to cast their votes in the contest.

This very carefully organised contest attracted and held interest continuously over a three month period right up to the last week, and the screening of the Coronation film. The town had been fairly well saturated with publicity in the form of hanging cards in shops, hotels, clubs and works canteens. 3,000 entry forms had been circulated, which also advertised the Coronation film. The cost of filming the children had been in the region of £80. In the words of a Rank Organisation representative, 'this was an object lesson on the meaning of showmanship where costs are a secondary consideration when a real victory is in sight'.

Without question the contest had been a huge success with over 6,250 votes being cast. The winner who polled 1,386 of those votes was Elizabeth Dunne of Johnson Square, Cherry Tree Terrace, Beverley. Second and third prizewinners were Elizabeth Ball, Keldgate with 780 votes and Judith Margaret Fryer, Westwood Road with 757 votes. ( over the years I have made repeated requests in an attempt to trace any surviving film from this event, unfortunately without success).

The popularity of the Playhouse midnight matinees continued, and in 1954 the proceeds were again to augment the funds for the Beverley Memorial Hall, and although the programmes had been chosen to attract varied audiences at the late hour, one of the more successful films was the British production, 'Great Expectations' ( 1948, Dir: David Lean ). Included as a supporting film on this occasion was local news of the launching of the 'George Irwin' at the Beverley shipyard, filmed by Ernest in 1953.

Another local news film supporting not just the usual programme, but also a midnight matinee, was a film taken by Ernest of the location work being carried out by the Ealing Film Studios for their production of 'Lease of Life' ( 1954, Dir: Charles Frend ).

For this production, Beverley Minster was converted into a giant film studio for a few days so as to obtain important interior shots. I vividly remember as a child being taken round the Minster to view the production with cameras, lights and with an occasional peep at the stars, Robert Donat, Kay Walsh, and Adrienne Corri. I was fascinated to see a film being made. It certainly generated tremendous interest for many people not just in Beverley but at the other major location of Lund. I was fortunate in being able to acquire a copy of this short newsreel film showing the location work at the Minster, for my own collection.

Mid-year 1954 brought the Sunday Cinema opening issue back into the news again. A Sunday Cinema Association had been formed with the manager of the Regal, Mr. Archie Heaton, acting as secretary. The first step taken by the Association was to organise a door-to-door canvass to ascertain public feeling. Their efforts were rewarded when a petition containing 5,311 signatures was presented to the Council.

The battle for a Sunday opening was to continue for many months yet. Some supporters even doubted a favourable outcome, but from March 13th, 1955 the first licence for Sunday Cinema was granted to the Regal Cinema, with the following conditions: 5% of the gross takings (after entertainment tax had been deducted) had to be given to two charities, namely The Royal Cancer Hospital Research Fund, and The British Spastic Society, both to receive equal portions, and no children under the age of 15 were to be admitted without an adult accompanying them. As for staff no-one who had worked on the previous six days continuously could work on the seventh day. However, although a Sunday licence was granted to the Playhouse in April 1955 there were no immediate intentions to hold Sunday evening performances.

On November 20th, 1954, the 'Beverley Guardian' carried a headline proclaiming 'New Screen at Local Cinema'. This referred to the introduction of Cinemascope at the Playhouse. This new screen was a 'curved translucent glass mirror type'. 'The anamorphic process is manifested through the latest system, called 'Del Rama.' In non-technical terms, what this means is a wider curved screen installed to reproduce, from a squeezed image on the film, a picture approximately 2½ times as wide as it is deep. The 'Del Rama' was, in actual fact, a pair of mirrors. The first receiving the image was concave, the second and lower one being convex thus spreading the picture unsqueezed out to fill the screen. The overall effect was very impressive. (I always enjoyed films in this process as I felt it created more of an illusion of involvement).

The first film produced in Cinemascope was 'The Robe' (1953, Dir: Henry Koster), and was presented at the Playhouse on Monday, November 22nd 1954, at the official opening ceremony under the patronage of the Mayor and Mayoress (Councillor and Mrs. Geoff Scruton), members of the Council, officials of the Beverley Corporation, George Odey, Esq., M.P. for Beverley division, and clergy of all denominations. The event was a huge success. Mr. Odey paid tribute to Ernest, praising his pioneering spirit in the film industry, and mentioning the many 'firsts' he had introduced to the town — the first permanent theatre to show silent films, and later talking films, films in colour, and of course the very important 'local news' which had brought so much pleasure to so many. And what of the Cinemascope presentation? The results were 'scintillated with brilliance and sheer beauty of colour. Some of the scenes were highly stereoscopic'.

January 1955 brought to the Playhouse screen the now-completed and eagerly-awaited 'Lease of Life'. Unfortunately, negotiations for securing this film had not been easy. The satisfactory outcome had only resulted from Ernest's direct approaches to J. Arthur Rank himself. Reading some of the correspondence involved, it appears that there had been quite a battle over the acquisition of 'Lease of Life'. On Monday, January 24th, 'Lease of Life' opened at the Playhouse to a curious and very interested audience comprising many who had been involved in not just the film itself as extras, but those who had accommodated the film crews, and seen to the catering, along with others who had watched the various stages of the film's production. The film was a huge success in Beverley, or 'Gilchester' as it was known in the film, and played to packed houses. I don't recall seeing the film at the time of release, but on the numerous television screenings I have been fascinated by some of the studio interior shots showing the Minster through windows in the background at angles I can never quite place in relation to surrounding properties. It is obvious that they must have been large photographs of the Minster placed behind the windows. It was good to see Beverley Minster taking a leading role along with the stars.

In April of the same year, Ernest wrote to the 'Beverley Guardian' a letter briefly outlining the new techniques for motion picture production and presentation mentioning the now well-established Cinemascope, and Paramount's new process VistaVision. VistaVision claimed 'Motion Picture High Fidelity'. To explain this briefly, VistaVision was 35mm film running horizontally in the camera producing an improved quality negative twice the normal frame size. For general use this could by printed by reduction on to standard 35mm film retaining the original quality from this larger negative, but for special presentations quality contact copies could be obtained from the master negative. In VistaVision-equipped cinemas the film could be projected horizontally on special projectors.

The first film in the VistaVision process was 'White Christmas' (1958, Dir: Michael Curtiz) and it promised to be startling in clarity, detail and realism. I have vivid memories of one of those 'White Christmas' screenings at the Playhouse when, having to sit on the front row of the front stalls, I discovered that screens had holes in them! I was so close that I could have counted them. Nevertheless I'm sure the picture did look clearer, even at that closeness, but probably the thing I remember most was the way that the middle 'V' in VistaVision came to the front of the picture first from the Paramount mountain, followed by 'Vista' and 'ision' to form the complete word. It was different, and to me it looked good.

I began to think that the novelty of Playhouse competitions had worn off until in my researches I came across a 'close-shave' competition. The competition was open to everyone who had experienced a close shave, a narrow escape, or some other happening of that nature, and if the judges thought your story combined the 'elements of adventure and chance' you were the winner, as was Mr. J. Waites, a gardener of Lairgate. His story told of how, at the age of 16, as a farm labourer, he was driving two horses and a wagon load of straw into the foldyard when he suddenly felt himself slipping forward. Hitting his head on the wagon pole, he found himself under the horses' feet with the wagon still moving. Mr. Waites said, 'I felt the front wheel touch my body. I gritted my teeth. For a moment I thought, 'I'm done'. Then, the whole lot stopped dead. The reins had jammed under the other wheel and stopped the horses, saving him from death or serious injury. Mr. Waites won hands down. The judges, advertising agents of Ronson Products, said 'His experience certainly must have been most frightening'. Mr. Waites was presented with his prize of a Ronson Electric Shaver at a ceremony in the Playhouse by Mrs. Helen Lewis, the Women's column editor of the 'Beverley Guardian'.

Sadly, by late 1956, Ernest's health was deteriorating. His heart trouble and associated complications were cause for concern and his visits to the Playhouse became a struggle. This is probably the reason for finding no record of other competitions or of any further films made by Ernest in 1955 or 1956.

In the 'Beverley Guardian' dated Saturday, February 2nd, 1957 a letter was published from Ernest paying tribute to his Chief Projectionist, Mr. Bill Jones, who had died suddenly on the previous Thursday. Ernest's great respect for Bill, not just as an employee but as a friend, was made obvious through these words. Ernest and the Playhouse had lost a friend who could never by replaced. Sadly, Ernest never saw his tribute to Bill in print because he passed away himself before the 'Beverley Guardian' was delivered at his home in Eastgate, Beverley, on Saturday, February 2nd 1957. He was 74.

In his address at the service in the Minster, the Reverend Reginald Hargreaves made reference to the many people 'who will recall occasions when they have thanked Ernest for some act of kindness and generosity'. A fellow Rotarian expressed the feelings of his colleagues by saying, 'Ernest Symmons was the kindest man I ever met!' I have, throughout my years of association with the Playhouse, heard these sentiments echoed many times, and I am confident Ernest will be especially remembered for a long time for both his kindness and generosity to the people of Beverley and district.

With Ernest gone, people were soon wondering what would happen to the Playhouse. His widow Thelma was quick to allay their fears through a letter to the 'Beverley Guardian' assuring the cinemagoers that with permission of the Licencing Authorities, the show would go on. The show did go on for quite a few more years as you will discover.

During September 1957 came an announcement that Thelma Symmons would be opening the Playhouse every Sunday evening, offering patrons new and popular old films, especially those that had been requested, and promised that personal service which had always given the Playhouse such a friendly atmosphere.

Early in 1958 the Marble Arch Cinema started having the occasional stage-show on Wednesday nights, one star turn being Norman Collier. I'm not sure if these shows replaced the film programme or supplemented it, although I feel this move was a brave attempt to attract a few of the rapidly-growing television viewers from their firesides to re-visit the cinema.

Cinema attendances were falling. During the first quarter of 1958 they had totalled 199 million, but were about 65 million or 24% below the corresponding period for the previous year. There had been a seasonal increase but the bad weather during February and March was blamed for a 'probable' drop in admissions; whatever the excuse, no-one could escape the fact that cinema audiences were on the decline.

Television had to be the reason. It had brought 'small screen cinema' into the home. The industry had made many ambitious attempts to fight back in the early fifties with large and wide screen systems such as Cinerama, Todd A.O., VistaVision and the popular Cinemascope, including systems from many different companies, with names such as Dyaliscope, Hammerscope, Naturama, Reglascope, Spectascope and Warnerscope to mention a few. These were all basically the same as Cinemascope and afforded the attraction of wide-screen cinema. Even with the added dimension of Stereophonic sound the advancing tide of television could not be slowed.

Midnight matinees continued to be successful, and in the typical Symmons tradition, were organised to raise funds for some worthwhile charity or good cause. Two I came across in 1959 were 'A Hair in the Soup' (1957, Dir: Maurice Regamay), a French comedy sponsored by the local Inner Wheel Club in aid of Cancer Research funds; the second was again a French comedy, 'Fernandel the Dressmaker' (1956, Dir: Jean Boyer), with proceeds in aid of funds to build a new Methodist Church in Queens Road, Beverley (demolished in 1984). These late shows proved very popular and usually played to full houses.

Whatever the state of the cinemagoing public in Beverley, March was the month both the marble Arch and Regal cinemas announced their plans for their patrons' benefit. The Marble Arch had installed two new modern projectors, new rectifiers, 'Hi-Fi' sound equipment, and new seats in the circle, while at the other end of the town the Regal offered a 'bit extra' by starting to show two full-length feature films in each programme, enabling patrons to see 3½ hour programmes.

And what was happening at the Playhouse? May 1959 brought quite a lengthy programme lasting almost 3 hours with Robert Donat's last film 'Inn of the Sixth Happiness' (1958, Dir: Mark Robson). A month later I saw Walt Disney's 'Fantasia' (1940), presented in SuperScope. As you may know, this film not only relies on its visuals to entertain, but is really a film about music, and being able to hear it well is of paramount importance. Now, if some of you can cast your minds back, you will recall that amusement fairs used to be held in the Market Place just outside the cinema. [10]

As will be appreciated the noise from the generators, dodgem cars, Noah's Ark etc., created quite a problem in the cinema. I tried hard to concentrate on the film, but even with the sound turned well up I was very much aware of the fairground activities, as I'm sure many people must have been over the years, until the fairground eventually moved to the Morton Lane car park.

If you have travelled this far through my book you will be well aware of the carnivals so popular during the thirties. In 1960, and as part of an effort to raise money for the new public baths, the carnival was revived, this time nothing to do with the Playhouse but the Regal, where on stage nightly was held the 'Carnival Queen' competition to choose a 'Miss Beverley 1960'; However, there was now no Ernest Symmons to record the event for the 'local news'.

Even though the newsreels and other films of local interest had long since ceased production, I was pleased to find they had not been forgotten, for during 1960 as a support to the Rock Hudson, Doris Day film 'Pillow Talk' (1959, Dir: Marty Melcher) found showing all the week was 'The Romance of Leather', the film made by Ernest of our once thriving leather industry.

[10] — and the evening I saw 'Fantasia' was such an occasion.

October brought an announcement in the 'Beverley Guardian' that the Playhouse was celebrating its '50th Anniversary Year — 1910-1960'. I couldn't believe my eyes. Had I made an error? Did the Playhouse really open in 1910 and not 1911 as I had discovered? I frantically searched the 1910 newspapers, and to my relief I found no announcement of the Playhouse opening. My date was correct. The Playhouse had opened on February 20th, 1911, and should have celebrated 50 golden years in 1961. So what was the reason for this difference of a year? I can only assume it was due to the fact that 1910-1960 sounded better than 1911-1961, as the earliest recorded information I can find relating to the lease acquirement was in the council minutes of January 27th, 1911, a letter from Debenham and Co., of York asking for the use of the Corn Exchange for exhibiting motion pictures.

Down at the Marble Arch one night in late October, a social session was being held offering a suprise item for patrons! (I wonder what it was). The following week on stage they offered a pop parade and quiz, thirty minutes of variety.

A week later they announced a speical attraction for patrons' pleasure, 'A Social Evening'. For 1/6 (7½p) one could see the film presentation ending at 8.45, then five minutes later at 8.50 until approximately 10.15 one could partake of the delights of the social activities, profits from which were donated to local charities. However, before the year ended the first sign of bingo 'broke out' at the Marble Arch under the title of 'Housey, Housey'. This was soon to spread and infect Beverley's two other cinemas over the next eight years.

*The Staff of the Playhouse Cinema, June 1931. Cyril Jenny, Bill Jones, Laurie Davies, Charlie Dixon, Brenton Symmons, Harry Jones, Mrs. Landen, Gertie Stroud, Drummer Helm, Thelma Monsen, Elaine Jenny and Mrs. Jenny.*

*Saturday Market and the Playhouse, December 1931.*

*Playhouse Staff outing, 1932.*

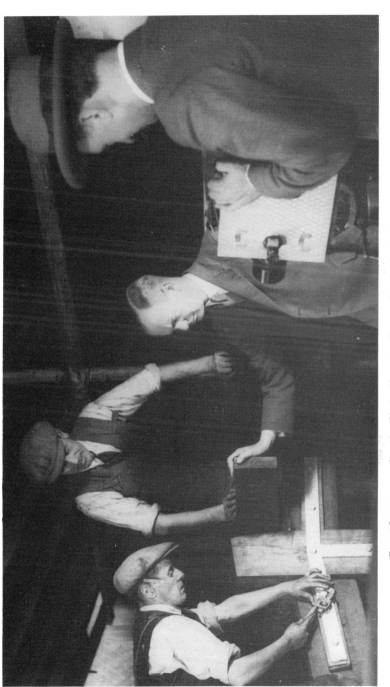

*Ernest Symmons on location filming the restoration work in St. Mary's Church, Beverley for the film, 'The Villain in the Wood', 1935.*

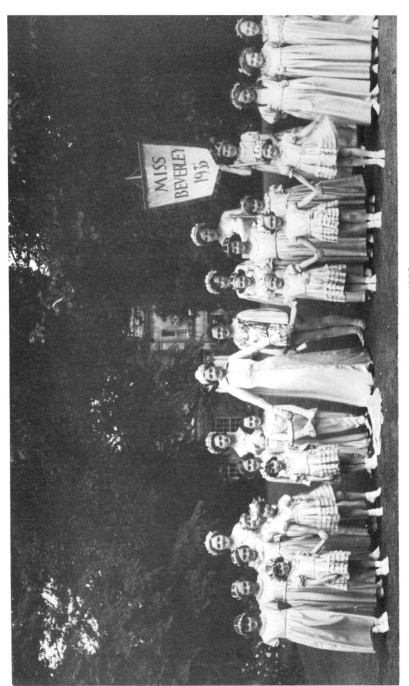

*The Miss Beverley competition, 1936.*

## The Last Event of the Week

IN AID OF THE HOSPITAL FUNDS.

### A WONDERFUL

# SUNDAY NIGHT CONCERT

### (SUNDAY, JULY 11th, 1937)

## At the PICTURE PLAYHOUSE,

At 8-0 p.m.          Doors open 7-30 p.m.

## ELMA CRAFT AND HER ACCORDIAN FOLLIES.

●●

## ROLAND FORD (B.B.C. Artist)

### and his Electric Hawaiian Guitar,

with HAROLD DAWSON at the Piano.

●●

## THE VAGABONDS CONCERT PARTY

CONNIE TODD, Contralto.
BERT TOPPING, at the Piano.
JOE NEWBOULD, Tenor.
ROBERT WISE, Bass Baritone.
SYLVIA, The Sophisticated Songstress.
DORIS ALLAN, Monologues, etc.
BERNARD CARTEN, Humorist and Compère.

—————— PRICES ——————

Reserved Seats, 2/-          Unreserved, 1/- & 6d.

Printed by Wright & Hoggard, Minster Press, Beverley.

*The last event in the programme for the 'Beverley through the Ages' pageant, July 1937.*

*The Craft Guilds, 'Beverley through the Ages', 1937.*

*Sanctuary — A scene from 'Beverley through the Ages', 1937*

*Fred Elwell, R.A., as Earl Hastings, carrying the sword of justice, 'Beverley through the Ages', 1937.*

*A scene from 'Beverley through the Ages', 1937.*

# CHAPTER FIVE

## Eyes Down

February 1961 brought to the Playhouse screen the classic Hitchcock thriller 'Psycho' (1960). Much excitement was generated around this film, mainly I think because 'No one . . . But no one' was admitted to the cinema after the start of each performance, and I seem to remember this rule being strictly enforced.

Meanwhile, back at the Marble Arch they had to cancel all their social evenings until further notice. I don't know what brought about this sudden change, but within a week Mr. Harry Popple [11] the manager presented a cheque to the Mayor, Councillor Harold Godbold for £167-19-9 (£167.99) as proceeds raised from the social evenings for local charities.

In July, Mr. Popple expressed regrets at having to stop his social evenings, but in response to popular demand 'The Marble Arch Social (Bingo) Club' had been formed. This was to be a members only club with all money from sale of tickets being returned as prizes. Bingo had arrived, with the Marble Arch holding three sessions weekly on Sundays, Tuesdays and Fridays. The Playhouse managed to hold bingo at bay for just over a year.

Carnivals continued to be a popular summer attraction in the town. As I had bought myself a standard 8 movie-camera a few years earlier I was still, in 1962, capturing practically anything that moved on film so the annual carnival was no exception. Although not equipped to the same standard as Ernest would have been with his very visible camera and tripod, I ventured forth with my camera, not much film stock, as it was quite expensive, but with plenty of enthusiasm. As producer, director, and cameraman I filmed as much of the occasion as possible before I ran out of film.

[11] Harry Popple joined the Marble Arch as a messenger boy when he left school. In 1927 he became a projectionist and eventually worked his way up to Chief Projectionist until, in 1941, he was 'called-up' and joined the RAF. However, a recall came through and he returned to the Marble Arch as Manager in 1942, and remained in that position until the cinema closed in 1967. Harry was, like Ernest, very much involved with charity work and is noted for his entertainment to the service personnel in the area, holding regular Sunday concerts during and after the War and raising over £3,000 for charity through his efforts. Tragically, like so many dedicated cinema managers, Harry had to succumb to the changing trends in leisure needs, being forced to forsake films for bingo. During this period the Marble Arch acquired the affectionate nick-name of 'Pop's Den', and I remember with a smile the bingo rhyming slang occasionally used for the number ten, 'Pop's Den number ten', later to become the more accepted 'Downing Street number ten'. However, Harry didn't lose his interest in films and the cinema as you will find out later.

I can't remember how I was encouraged to show my nine-minute epic at the Playhouse, but I do recall the first test screening one Saturday night after the film, 'Flower Drum Song' (1961, Dir: Henry Koster) having sat through it in anticipation of what my effort would look like on the big screen. I was pleasantly surprised. The 8mm projector was mounted in front of, and resting on, one of the cinema's 35mm projectors. The picture must have looked alright, for as a result of this private viewing, Mrs. Symmons invited me to screen the film publicly, twice nightly and three times on Saturday. I was amazed to see how good the quality was from that small standard 8 frame, projected over a distance of 74 feet, although it didn't quite fill the screen. To quote the 'Beverley Guardian', 'It is an extremely clear and well-edited piece of film. None of its detail or really excellent colour are lost, and it should not be missed.' Of course, the results could not be compared with those of a normal 35mm presentation, but with a specially-bought lens and 'souped up' lamp the results were acceptable. I attended the cinema for each performance of my film throughout the seven days, mainly because I was familiar with the projector, which made it easier for the projectionist to control the taped soundtrack. I didn't win an Oscar for my contribution to the film industry, but I did benefit from the experience. It had been good fun, and I had succeeded in reviving the 'local news'.

November brought a 'special midnight matinee' presented by the Beverley Lions Club, and according to the press they were 'breaking new ground' in presenting the French Revue 'Femmes De Paris', certificate X, which had been passed by the East Riding Watch Committee. This new screen revue straight from Paris offered spectacular entertainment for the broad-minded 'over 16's' (in 1962 you had to be 16 or over to see an 'X' certificate film, unlike the eighties when you should be 18!).

The entire proceeds from the event went in aid of the Lion Clubs charity works, and, as a large audience was anticipated, patrons were advised to 'book one of the 3/3 (16p) seats at the earliest possible moment'. Other seats were available at 1/9 (9p) and 2/9 (14p). The show was a huge success.

It was just eight years to the month since CinemaScope films were first shown at the Playhouse, the original Anamorphic 'Del-Rama' system was still in use. However, improvements were on the way, which I believe were the direct result of complaints of poor picture quality when 'Scope' films were shown.

Two Dyaliscope Anamorphic lenses were bought. These lenses would completely replace the original mirror system, and greatly improve the overall picture quality.

It had been decided that every effort would be made to get the new lenses operational for the opening night of the award-winning film 'Ben Hur' (1959, Dir: William Wyler). The 'best' and bookable seats were 5/- (25p), and if you had 2/6 (12½p) to spare there was an excellent souvenir programme available.

Numerous tests were made with the new lenses, but the biggest problem was mounting them, there was just no suitable way to fit them in front of the projectors.

Fortunately I had a colleague who was prepared to make numerous metal supports for us, but regardless of how well they were secured to the projectors the problem of vibration could not be eliminated. The chief projectionist was at a loss for a solution. 'Ben Hur' had started, and then I had an idea to suspend the lenses from the original 'Del-Rama' fittings and slide them across into position when required. It worked!

'The Beverley Guardian' carried the Playhouse advertisement, proudly announcing that the last two performances of the magnificent 'Ben Hur' would be perfectly projected through the new CinemaScope lenses. Seeing the final results made the effort all worthwhile.

Sadly, just over a month after the chariots from 'Ben Hur' had thundered across the Playhouse screen, a new sound was heard.

Bingo had arrived, introducing the new language of 'two little ducks; doctor's orders; 7/6 was she worth it?' and so on.

The Playhouse Bingo Club was formed with the opening session on Sunday afternoon, December 16th 1962. All the latest bingo apparatus had been installed in an effort to attract customers to this new club.

For Christmas 1962 bingo players, besides cash, had the chance of extra prizes including chickens and hampers and a cash snowball of £13 on 46 numbers!

At first I wasn't too keen on bingo. I feared its popularity, and the possible threat to the cinema — not just the Playhouse, but the Marble Arch and Regal too. However, as it didn't spill over from Sunday afternoons I was quite happy, and my only involvement with the bingo was the preparation after the show on Saturday nights erecting the stage and helping with all the other bits associated with the game. Everything had to be cleared away again before the Sunday night film.

One film I must mention is one of the all-time worsts, 'Plan 9 from Outer Space' (1959, Dir: Edward Wood Jr.). If you've seen it you know what I mean when I say, 'it's rough'. I sat patiently through this 'classic' totally confused and amazed at such an appalling film. At the end of the show I related my opinions to the projectionists who both laughed, adding that they had accidentally shown two reels in the wrong order. They had succeeded in making a bad film even worse.

Three weeks after the 'Plan 9' show came the end of Sunday night cinema, although I'm sure this had nothing to do with 'Plan 9' itself. Bingo had spilt over to Sunday nights and this, I feared, was 'the thin end of the wedge'. Admittedly, cinema audiences had dropped and without doubt bingo was rapidly growing in popularity.

In March 1963 bingo at the Playhouse had spread from Sunday afternoons and evenings to Mondays and Thursdays with the introduction of cine-bingo, and for 1/9 (9½p) it was now possible to see a film then stay on for bingo. To me this was a big mistake because not many bingo players were cinemagoers, so usually during the last thirty minutes of the film, hoardes of bingo players, not interested in the film, arrived thus spoiling it for those who were. I couldn't help wondering how long this could go on.

My interests in films and cinema didn't decline and neither did my interest in the Playhouse, so it was almost automatic that I became more involved in the social club activities with a degree of reluctance. By June, bingo fever had caused Saturday nights to switch to cine-bingo, so now, as well as the original Sunday afternoon bingo, cine-bingo occupied Sunday, Monday Thursday and Saturday nights, but you still had chance to see the film programme, without bingo interference on Tuesday, Wednesday, and Friday nights, and the Saturday matinee. It soon became obvious that bingo was here to stay. It came as no surprise when the 'Beverley Guardian' carried the headline, 'It will be Bingo only at the Playhouse'. Mrs. Symmons had told the press, 'It is with very real regret that we have come to this decision, but people have just stopped going to the cinema'. Films did not cease immediately, but carried on throughout the children's summer holidays. However, a closing date had been decided upon and the last film screened was Cliff Richard and the Shadows in 'Summer Holiday', (1963, Dir: Peter Yates), the final show being on Saturday, 7th September 1963. This show was not an event to be remembered, for as with all cine-bingo, the end was marred by the influx of bingo supporters. So ended 52 years of film entertainment at the Playhouse.

In August the question arose over the rent paid by Mrs. Symmons to the Council in view of the Playhouse being now used solely for bingo. Some felt the rent was too low, but as the then present lease still had three years to run, the rent had been fixed. Thankfully, some members of the committee expressed concern over the fact that Mrs. Symmons had been losing money over a long period of cinema operation, and had she continued would have gone out of business entirely. In conclusion it was felt that Mrs. Symmons should be allowed to recover some of the money she had lost.

If the latter years of cinema hadn't been paying, bingo certainly was as the social club audiences continued to expand aided by what was to become one of bingo's big attractions, not just in Beverley but throughout the country. It was the first 'National Golden Scoop', well remembered, I'm sure, by many. The 'Scoop' was always the first game of the evening, and although rather clumsy in its early days, soon became very sophisticated. Each night the club would phone a regional scoop office to be given a security code number relating to one of a sealed pack of pre-printed games. The envelope was opened before witnesses who scrutinised the whole game by sitting at the side of the bingo caller while he related the numbers in order as printed. The first person to claim a 'full house' in the least possible numbers was the winner. This same game would be played in the numerous participating clubs throughout the country. The purchase of the scoop tickets was divided between the participating club and the National organisers who, after each club had phoned their ticket sales value to the regional offices, could then start to assess the prize money to be awarded that night, and, as will be appreciated, the more clubs participating, the higher the prizes with the highest going to the lucky player who called 'house' on the lowest number that night. I hope readers who have never experienced bingo do not find this description too complicated:

As already mentioned, the 'National Golden Scoop' had very attractive cash prizes to be won nightly, so I feel it necessary to mention our first big win at the Playhouse. It's an occasion I remember well, for not only did the big money come to the Playhouse, but the old mill in Mill Lane suffered extensive damage as a result of a major fire. So intense was the heat that passing trains had to be sprayed with water. That event contributed to my memory of Mrs. Gorbutt winning the scoop prize of nearly £1,000 and the excitement it generated. Dear Mrs. Gorbutt remained so calm, but the rest of us were past ourselves with excitement. In a 'Beverley Guardian' interview later, Mrs. Gorbutt had said she 'prefers the Playhouse because of the friendliness of the patrons', and that is what, I'm sure, held the place together for so long. Those pioneering days of bingo were never to be repeated. The vast majority of the players went for a night out and to experience the wonderful companionship that bingo and the Playhouse afforded.

I can remember with great affection the wonderful sweet old lady customers who practically adopted me. (Of course, in those days I was a youngish lad!) The vast majority of our customers shared an incredible sense of humour with us, and how I recall with a smile Frank Elgey who, for no apparent reason, would suddenly have a fit of the giggles while he was calling. Frank had one of those infectious laughs, and the more he had to suppress it, the worse it became, and in no time at all, the audience was laughing and giggling with him.

Without doubt, to me the first five years were the best, for although bingo was a serious game, the membership was made up mainly of people who really enjoyed their social night out. At the Playhouse we had no bar, but this never affected the happy atmosphere. If anyone wanted a drink, they went out to the nearby pubs, either next door to the Push, to the Dog and Duck around the side, or across the market place to the King's Head or the Green Dragon. The only snag with the mass exodus for drinks at the interval was a race against time to get out for 'a quick one' and back before the next session, so the drinkers left through the nearest exit, which caused a problem in winter by taking the warm air out and letting the cold in, much to the annoyance of the remaining customers.

Even though I'd lost my film entertainment at the Playhouse, I was still able to enjoy visits to both the Regal and Marble Arch. I remember seeing James Bond in 'From Russia with Love' (1963, Dir: Terence Young) at the Regal and 'The Longest Day' (1962, Dir: Ken Annakin, Andre Marton, Bernhard Wicki) at the Marble Arch. The latter film stuck in my mind, not because the English part of the film was directed by Beverley born Ken Annakin; nor because it was three hours long; and not because it was screened for three weeks. It was simply that I hadn't been to the Marble Arch for quite a while and had forgotten the steep rake of the balcony. Memories came flooding back of how, as a child, I'd believed we saw the films before the people downstairs, because you couldn't see an audience below. How I can laugh at that occasion now.

I continued to enjoy my visits to the Regal and Marble Arch cinemas for quite some time until one day, out of the blue, the Marble Arch announced their complete switch to bingo. Like the Playhouse, there wasn't much fuss. Films ceased with the last showing of Elvis Presley in 'It happened at the World's Fair' (1963, Dir: Norman Taurog) on Saturday, May 15th 1964. From the following day, Whit Sunday, the Marble Arch would open six nights a week, except Wednesdays, for bingo offering greatly improved attractions and a Jumping Jackpot of £100. Meanwhile, down at the Playhouse, we offered two £60 jackpots, and a week later the Marble Arch offered not just the Jumping Jackpot, but a Junior Jackpot of £60 as well, proclaiming that 'all roads lead to Pop's Den'.

The competition between the two clubs became quite fierce. Of course, whichever one had the highest jackpot on the highest numbers attracted the most customers until won, then business dropped like a stone in water. Now, as you will appreciate, it was of great importance to know what the other club was doing or planning. Sometimes the customers would talk, or with a bit of persuasion, (friendly of course) be encouraged to inform us of happenings down the road. Fear not; it worked both ways, and both clubs had their 'Mata Hari's'. I don't think they ever received payment, but I suppose their expenses may have been paid. The whole spying situation was really comical, mainly because each club knew each other's agents, their usual giveaway being the way they could be seen to make notes on the back of their bingo books. All this may sound quite funny, but I assure you, this 'Bingo Espionage' was rife.

As the rivalry between the two social clubs continued, no opportunity was missed by either side to proclaim their virtues to the bingo playing public. The Playhouse announced that by 6th June 1964, £4,230 had been paid to lucky winners at the Playhouse in just over a year since the Scoop started. We also offered a 6d (2½p) Double Chance game — quickie — and special prizes to be won weekly whilst the Marble Arch offered the chance of no less than six jackpots. Advertisements carried the slogan

'Happy Harry calls the numbers — You collect the cash'.

In the 'Beverley Guardian' for July 17th, 1964 a report and photograph appeared covering a presentation to Mrs. Thelma Symmons of a nest of tables. This was to mark the appreciation by members of the Beverley Rotary and Inner Wheel Clubs for the work done over many years by Thelma and her late husband Ernest. The presentation was made at a cocktail party by Rotarian R. B. Booth, President of the Rotary Club, and Mrs. A. C. Millest, President of the Inner Wheel Club. Appreciation was expressed for the many shows that had been organised for the various charities, and how after Ernest's death Thelma had offered the Playhouse and its staff for many charity performances.

Even though I was involved with the bingo operations at the Playhouse I never lost my thirst for films, so I continued to be satisfied with frequent visits to our only cinema the Regal, and remember seeing such films as 'Zulu' ( 1963, Dir: Cy Endfield ), the award-winning 'Tom Jones' ( 1963, Dir: Tony Richardson ), [12] and two of my favourite films 'The Last Voyage' ( 1960, Dir: Andrew L. Stone ) and 'The Time Machine' ( 1960, Dir: George Pal ). I frequently wondered just how long the Regal could keep going, for it was obvious that their audiences were slowly slipping away, while bingo audiences continued to expand.

On New Years Day 1965, the Marble Arch proudly announced that they would open nightly except Wednesday, and boldly stated 'Play in Comfort — With Confidence'. That was the last announcement from the Marble Arch, for they suddenly ceased operations. I cannot recall the actual events surrounding this closure, but seem to think the whole affair was shrouded in an air of mystery.

Rumour, ( always rife in bingo halls ), had it that the Marble Arch was to be modernised and re-opened as a super bingo hall. Nothing much happened for a few months other than the Marble Arch regulars reluctantly coming to play bingo at the Playhouse.

On March 12, 1965 the 'Beverley Guardian' put a temporary stop to the rumour by reporting that the former cinema had been purchased by Mr. William Isaac for a Hull development company. There was no further news. At the Playhouse we waited with baited breath not knowing what to expect next.

We continued to entertain and amuse our supporters, holding them captive while they played for two £60 jackpots, the Golden Scoop and special prizes of a refrigerator and spin-dryer.

On this occasion the rumour was right. On May 7th, 1965 the 'Beverley Guardian' announced the opening of 'The New Marble Arch Bingo Club' re-opening with the tempting offer of '3 fabulous Jackpots of £100, £50 and £50 plus a chance to win a 4 day holiday in Paris, the whole occasion

[12] This is a film I feel played a very important part in the Playhouse story, but you will have to wait until 1972 to find out more.

59

being hosted by 'Happy Harry Popple'. Well, as bingo players do they followed the money, so off many went to the 'new club'; after all, they were offered enjoyment and a friendly atmosphere in the newly decorated, centrally heated club. The cash temptations came fast and furious. The month of May offered guaranteed minimum prize money each night of £32-15-0 (£32.75), and a Gala night each Thursday with free gifts, novelties and lots of fun, together with jackpots of £200 on 43 numbers, £100 on 47 numbers and £50 on 51 numbers. There were also super prizes to be won like an electric sewing maching, a fabulous radio, and a mystery prize worth £20!

The following month brought David Whitfield in person to the Marble Arch to sing a selection of old and new songs accompanied by Bert Gaunt at the piano, plus lots of free gifts including poultry and pop records presented by David Whitfield. Admission to this great event was 5/- (25p) and 7/6 (37½p), and you were advised to book your seats early. At the Playhouse, thankfully, we had built up and retained our core of regular supporters. On July 23rd we announced that we had three more Golden Scoop wins during the week; they were not thousands, just small runner-up prizes, but were nevertheless very valuable in promoting playing the Scoop at the Playhouse.

Down the road the opposition offered a special prize of a three-piece suite valued at £50, and if you fancied a trip to Bridlington you could accompany the children on their day trip to the seaside.

The following week we were proud to announce that since the Golden Scoop game started we had 86 wins with a total prize money amounting to £6,214-18-6d (£6,214.92½p). A week later it was up to 88 wins bringing the impressive cash win record up to £6,308-10-6d (£6,308.52½p).

At the Marble Arch it was time for a 'special added attraction' in the form of the 'Bob Roberts Show', members being invited to participate in this 'snappy' twenty minute show to test their skill to win cash prizes and free gifts.

During this period, to support my real interest which was in films, I would occasionally visit one of the Hull cinemas, but this was only for special big screen presentations like the first time I saw 'Lawrence of Arabia' (1962, Dir: David Lean) at the ABC Cinema with stereophonic sound, and at 10/6 (52½p) per seat. However, that was in 1964, but I still found this David Lean epic was equally impressive on the smaller screen when it eventually reached Beverley Regal in 1965. 'Lawrence', 'From Russia With Love', 'Goldfinger' (1964, Dir: Guy Hamilton), '633 Squadron' (1964, Dir: Walter E. Grauman), and that classic re-run of Walt Disney's 'Snow White and the Seven Dwarfs' are just a few of the good films that I can remember attracting decent audiences.

Christmas in the bingo halls was usually quite a jolly affair and invariably offered extra games and raffles. Mrs. Symmons and the Playhouse were noted for their really good Christmas activities mainly because the prizes were excellent and in plenty, usually comprising poultry, wines, spirits and other seasonal goodies. I don't ever recall them not attracting good crowds because of course, Christmas was the time of year when that windfall of cash was very welcome, so extra cash prizes were an added bonus.

Amidst all the festive excitement surrounding Christmas at the Clubs, I found the Marble Arch was, in December 1965, playing for a luxurious three-piece suite with a value of £50. This amused me for since July they had been playing special games almost weekly for a three-piece suite value £50. (except the Christmas '65 one was 'luxurious'!).

At the Playhouse we announced that our Scoop prize money won to date had been £7,800. The Christmas and New Year film entertainment offered by the Regal was quite reasonable with Disney's 'Davy Crockett — King of the Wild Frontier' (1955, Dir: Norman Foster), 'Babes in Toyland' (1961, Dir: Jack Donohue), 'The Legend of Young Dick Turpin' (1964, Dir: James Neilson), and that great comedy-western with Lee Marvin 'Cat Ballou' (1965, Dir: Elliot Silverstein).

As the months rolled by and our customers continued to have the good fortune to win 'little and often' on the Scoop game, we looked forward to the day we would reach £10,000. Sure enough, in May 1966 we had the pleasure of announcing that £10,000 had been won be the many lucky winners playing at the Playhouse. By December the figures had reached the magnificent sum of £12,132-17-2d (£12,132.87p).

1967 opened with an admission increase at both the Playhouse and Marble Arch from 2/- (10p) to 2/6 (12½p). The Marble Arch also introduced Super Colour Bingo. This is a rapid game played on illuminated boards, and in the early days cost only 6d (2½p) to play, offering a choice from over 500 prizes consisting mainly of tinned foodstuffs. The game was very popular, usually played before the main session bingo, during the interval and at the end of session.

I have to admit to being very surprised that we at the Playhouse didn't follow suit.

Meanwhile at the Regal I caught what I thought were some really good films: 'The Trap' (1959, Dir: Norman Panama), 'The Fantastic Voyage' (1966, Dir: Richard Fleischer), 'My Fair Lady' (1964, Dir: George Cukor), 'The Great Race' (1965, Dir: Blake Edwards). I remember attending the matinee performance of 'The Great Race', sadly I was the only one on the balcony to laugh at this comedy but that did not spoil my enjoyment. Shortly after this the Regal presented a great 'X' certificate week screening two 'X' films a night for six nights. One I have vivid memories of was 'The Night of the Demon' (1957, Dir: Jacques Tourneur), which really scared me, so much so that I walked home a different and long way so as to avoid a long dark passage.

The 'Beverley Guardian' dated May 5th, carried the headline 'Another Supermarket for Beverley? This referred to the Marble Arch (which had originally been sold in 1965 at auction for £13,500) and although there were no definite plans, the property had been bought by Moore's Stores Ltd., of Newcastle. Members were assured that entertainment would continue until such time as the company had their plans approved and were ready to move in.

Press advertisements advised members of the Marble Arch Social Club to look out for future activities of the club. The last advertisement appeared on August 11th, 1967, and I'm afraid I don't know if it closed or not, for between ourselves in the Market Place and the Marble Arch in Butcher Row a new luxury club opened in Toll Gavel called the 'Bambi'. Bingo players were invited to 'come up and see Pop sometimes'. This new club had opened with Harry Popple at the helm. I do not recall their opening having any adverse affect on our business, but it still represented competition so we had to keep on our toes. We once again announced our Scoop wins to date. By November the grand figure was £14,259-5-7 (£14,259.28½p), and whilst we offered a £149 snowball, the new Bambi offered a £250 jackpot.

At the Regal, Christmas and the year went out quietly and pleasantly with a good offering of Disney films, namely 'Snow White and the Seven Dwarfs', and 'The Lady and The Tramp' (1955, Dir: Hamilton Luske, Clyde Geronimi & Wilfred Jackson).

I seem to remember around this time the Regal starting to promote live groups on stage on Sunday nights before the film programme. Unfortunately, I am unable to find or trace in the press anything about these shows, but remember wondering at the time, whether this would herald the shape of things to come as had happened previously at the Marble Arch. I didn't have long to wait to find out.

The quiet before the storm probably summed up the Christmas 1967, film offerings. 1968 opened with 'Bonnie and Clyde' (1967, Dir: Arthur Penn), 'You Only Live Twice' (1967, Dir: Lewis Gilbert), and 'The Dirty Dozen' (1967, Dir: Robert Aldrich). On May 31st, the storm broke with the announcement that Beverley's youngest and last cinema would be closing and going over to full-time bingo from July.

A month after this 'knee shaking' announcement, we at the Playhouse introduced the very popular Colour or Prize Bingo, and I remember the occasion whilst speaking to the Regal manager Mr. Arnold Atkinson, when he said that he was very surprised at our installation of prize bingo in view of their opening in a few weeks.

They had planned to cease cinema operations on June 22nd, 1968, but I am very thankful they didn't for it gave me the chance to see Disney's 'The Jungle Book' (1967, Dir: Wolfgang Reitherman) (not once but three times). However, during the weeks before closure extensive alterations could be seen in progress.

The cinema closure came on Saturday, July 13th, with the last film 'Up The Junction' (1968, Dir: Peter Collinson), and the last Minors' Matinee on Saturday, July 6th, was 'Old Mother Riley Joins Up' (1939, Dir: Maclean Rogers). For this, their last show, the children were all admitted free of charge. Beverley had finally lost its film entertainment. We were now completely without a cinema for the first time in 57 years, so for cinemagoers like myself we were now forced into Hull, Driffield or Pocklington.

The Regal proclaimed its grand opening with half page adverts in the local press, and went on to open on Thursday, July 25th 1968, offering a free £100 game and free £25 draw for the holder of the lucky membership number.

In competition the Playhouse offered an £80 snowball on 51 numbers. We had expected to be empty, especially as the new opposition was offering three nights of free entrance admission. Surprise, Surprise! A good core of our regulars stuck by us and continued to do so for many years to come.

In August demolition started on the Marble Arch, and within a matter of weeks a memorial to 52 years of cinema was gone. So ended the Marble Arch Cinema. All that remains are memories. The site is now occupied by the Presto supermarket.

Harry Popple, ex-manager of the Marble Arch, had by now been appointed to manage the Criterion Cinema, George Street, Hull, and did so until its closure on June 4th, 1969. In December 1968, at the Playhouse we once again proudly announced our Scoop wins to date. Our total had now reached £17,212-13-0 (£17,212.65p). This was a particularly impressive figure to boast in front of our opposition, especially as they had no involvement with the 'National Golden Scoop'.

Out of curiosity a colleague from the Playhouse and I went along to the Regal for a game of bingo, and what a sad affair it was. So many of our once regular customers and 'friends' chose to ignore us. We did take note of what was going on, but I must admit to being very disillusioned by the way peoples attitudes had changed with the opening of this new club. On many occasions I feared for our future with competition being so fierce from the opposition, but Mrs. Symmons very bravely led us on through many a crisis. This was most apparent when 'they' had special attractions which would draw our customers their way, and Mrs. S, as we called her, did her level best to extend a very friendly and warm welcome through her paybox window to all who came, regular or not. I am confident our business succeeded for so many years through her never ending pleasantness and courtesy to all the members. Thankfully, a few of the staff had the same attitude as Mrs. S. This was often commented upon when people compared the two clubs.

Changes were ahead for all involved with gaming. New acts were introduced which prevented us from advertising in the press; we had to stop displaying our cash prize values outside the premises for all to see, the Golden Scoop was declared illegal for what seems a silly reason: the money won had to be paid out on the same night and try as the clubs might, even dating winners' cheques on the winning night couldn't solve this problem. In addition, gaming tax was introduced neatly 'nibbling' a bit out of the prize money paid to winners.

When 'link' games between clubs became viable and the Regal linked up with others in their circuit, we at the Playhouse 'teetered on the edge' never venturing into a link, and whilst in the early eighties the matter was considered in great detail, a link never materialised.

In the 'Beverley Guardian' dated July 31st 1970, two letters were published. Their message was simple — Why can't we have a cinema? Beverley had been without a cinema now for just two years, and many people, myself included, missed that local film entertainment. An approach had been made to the new tenants of the Regal, the Star Group of Companies, with the request for the possible return of cinema to the town. The answer was straight and to the point: they had proposed to introduce films three nights a week, but their landlords, Associated British Cinemas, refused permission. That wasn't the end of the matter for the 'Beverley Guardian' ran a plebiscite on August 21st. The results were published under the headline, 'Overwhelming Response on our Plebiscite. Over 830 vote for return to cinema', and not a single person voted against the idea of having films back in the town. The results were passed to the Star Group of Companies, who assured us that a 'fresh approach' would be made, accompanied by appropriate copies of the 'Guardian'. We never saw a return of films to the 'Regal' but that wasn't quite the end.

November 5th, 1971, saw a proud announcement from the 'Beverley Guardian': 'Guardian campaign gets films again'. Harry Popple was the man responsible for this move. Harry had managed the town's Memorial Hall for just over a year and thought this offered a challenge. Initially, the films were planned fortnightly on Sunday nights, the first show being on Sunday, November 7th. The opening film was John Wayne in 'Chisum' (1970, Dir: Andrew V. McLaglen). [13] The admission was only 25p and 15p for children under 14 and senior citizens. The first show was a huge success, some people being turned away. Through the 'Beverley Guardian' we were invited to submit details of the type of films we would like to see at the Memorial Hall.

Although the shows were well supported at first, after a few weeks, the audiences started to fall. This tragic development was due, I think, to the very poor acoustics of the Memorial Hall. I had thankfully seen most of the films so knew what was going on, but for those who hadn't I doubt if they

[13] I would like to add that the quality of these shows was of a very high standard, all of the films being on the 16mm gauge.

could hear a word being said as the dialogue, no matter how loud, just seemed to 'bounce' around. I believe this inability to hear well was a contributing cause to the restlessness and rowdyism amongst the audience. The seats did not help either, and anyone who has ever sat on them for any more than half an hour will know the feeling (or lack of it!). Harry Popple did his level best to maintain order but with little success. On one occasion the police were called in an attempt to reduce the noise. In my opinion, the Memorial Hall just did not, and still does not, lend itself to film entertainment. For some shows as few as thirty people had turned up. I was amused by one of the operators' comments that the James Bond film, 'Thunderball' (1965, Dir: Terence Young) would have done better business, and I'm sure it would have done, had it not been almost an hour late in arriving. I recall there had been an enormous queue at opening time, but it soon dwindled. After all, who wants to wait around on a cold February night? Eventually we were allowed inside to sit and wait for the arrival of our show, but this meant extra time on those hard seats.

It wasn't long, therefore, before the inevitable happened. The 24th March, 1972 'Beverley Guardian' headline read, 'It's shutdown for the Cinema'. Financial loss through lack of support had brought about the closure of the cinema, less than five months after its opening. The Dewsbury-backed operation said that the takings had been bad to say the least, and on occasions had not met the cost of the film, let alone the advertising and the hire of the hall. With the Memorial Hall failure and the loss of three cinemas, I resigned myself to never being able to experience cinema or see films again in Beverley. However, this is not the end of my story, but more a beginning.

# CHAPTER SIX

## A New Light

Just around the time the Memorial Hall shows were ending, I purchased a 16mm projector as a progressive stage in my hobby, although at the time I had no specific use intended for it; then one night after a bingo session, Mrs. Symmons, a member of staff, Wendy Harrison, and myself were sitting talking about the sad loss of films in the town. Wendy said how wonderful it would be to see them again at the Playhouse. Mrs. S. and myself both agreed.

I started thinking that if a film cost about £20 to hire it would only require 20 people paying one pound each, 40 paying 50p or 80 paying 25p and so on. The more I thought about the possibility of bringing films back to the Playhouse, the more enthusiastic I became. I thought about forming a club, a group, or a film appreciation society, after all, I had my new 16mm projector what else could I possibly need!?

At this point I would like to introduce you to two good friends, Adrian Moore and Aubrey Goodyear, both of whom were instrumental in the development of the film society and the re-introduction of film to the town. Both of them liked my idea, but would it work? How could we possibly succeed when three cinemas and the Memorial Hall had failed?

I discussed the idea with Mrs. Symmons. Thankfully she approved and gave me her blessing. I inserted a couple of postcards in Simsons Pet Shop display case inviting anyone with an interest in forming a film appreciation society to contact me. I don't think there were any replies.

In the meantime Adrian, Aubrey and myself had set about testing the suitability of my projector and screen (a screen was necessary as the old cinema one was covered with polythene and curtains, and as such was unusable).

The projection set up worked well, as I had expected, but that was only using my 50″ × 40″ screen. This would of course restrict the number of people able to sit and view in comfort, so an alternative would have to be found.

On April 28th, 1972 my advertisement appeared in the 'Beverley Guardian' again inviting anyone interested in helping to form a film appreciation society to contact me. Still not much interest was shown until one of the newspaper staff read my advertisement, and after a long talk gave me front page editorial space with the heading 'Film "sequence" is still

Running'. As a result of this my worries over possibly getting started were eased. Two school teachers were the first to come forward; David Barwick who was to become our first secretary, and John Killen, who became and remained our Chairman for the full 9½ years of operation.

One day, while in the newsagents, I was attracted to a copy of 'Punch'. The cover was a montage of films. I picked it up and flicked through it, finding right at the back an article on forming a film society. This was just what we needed — who to contact and what to do to keep within the law. This was when I realised I would need more than just a screen — and my 16mm projector.

As advised I contacted the British Federation of Film Societies who provided me with all the information I needed to keep the operation legal. Firstly we had to have a constitution before we could be accepted, and register as a film society. No charge for admission could be made at the door, none of the officers could receive any payment for their services (legitimate expenses were allowed) and probably the most important consideration was safety. We had to protect our potential patrons as per the part of the Cinematograph Act regarding premises used only occasionally for the cinematograph exhibitions.

I began to get cold feet. Everything now seemed so complicated. Before the Federation would accept us as a fully affiliated society, we had to have a committee comprising of a group of responsible people. So far we had organised ourselves very well. John Killen as Chairman; David Barwick as Secretary; Aubrey Goodyear as technical adviser; Adrian Moore as theatre manager, and me? I volunteered to be the projectionist. We were just one officer short — we needed a treasurer. Gently an approach was made to my Aunt, Violet Rose (the one who took me to the cinema so often when I was a child), with a plea for her to be our treasurer. Eventually she was persuaded to hold our purse-strings (although at this time there was nothing in it). Violet thankfully kept our finances straight throughout all our years of operation.

Interest was beginning to grow in our activity, so the committee started thinking seriously about getting some members to put some money into what was perhaps a bit of a hair-brained idea. As we gained momentum, I realised that the lease on the cinema was only a couple of years off expiration, and as with most of the lease applications there was nearly always a doubt over its renewal. However, I thought whatever the future held it would be good to see the Playhouse go out as it started — showing films. I remember voicing these thoughts aloud one night to one of my bingo colleagues. His answer was not one to inspire confidence. He simply said: 'Films will never save this place'. How wrong he was proved on more than one occasion.

I cannot begin to express my appreciation to the 'Beverley Guardian' and a young reporter, Jeremy Ashcroft-Hawley. He was a pillar of strength in his interest and encouragement, even to the point of printing on the front page of the 'Guardian' full details of what we attempted to offer and an application form for membership. We had agreed to operate on a six-month season basis, screening eight films each season. I had calculated that if I set a target of 150 members all paying a subscription of £1.50 each in advance, the £225 would cover the estimated film hire and hopefully cover additional expenses.

We decided to restrict membership to 150 mainly because each member was entitled to purchase a guest ticket in advance of the show, and I had fears of a possible turn out on some occasions of 300 members and guests, and although we had the seats, the proposed new screen position would not allow acceptable viewing to that number of people.

Occasionally, I had feelings this just couldn't work, and feared accepting money as the memberships started to roll in, but felt slightly comforted by my promises in the 'Guardian' to refund their cash if the venture failed through lack of support.

Our first commitee meeting was to choose the first season of films. Each committe member chose one film the remaining films being a joint decision. For our first season we selected our films from the Film Distributors Associated catalogue. This company allowed a generous block booking discount of 25% off the catalogue price of each film, provided, of course, we booked a minimum of eight within a year. (Their prices, after discount, ranged between nine and fifteen pounds).

The films we chose were not quite what film societies were expected to show. The titles were very commercial. However, our nearest cinema was eight miles away in Hull, so we posed no serious threat to them.

With the film-booking out of the way, (a task I was to be responsible for throughout our years of operation) we had to start work on the practical side. Firstly, a new screen was required. We had no money in the kitty to spare, so I ordered and paid for a 10' × 8' roller screen. In due course it arrived, and what a problem it caused. It was so well packed that approximately an extra foot was added to its length. On my arrival home for lunch I was greeted with this 'monstrosity' sticking out of the front door. On inspection inside, the other end was neatly laid across the loo floor. A decision was quickly made for the screen's removal. So, not having a car available, I set off to walk to town carrying the screen. I remember well it was a warm windy day, and I had great difficulty turning corners, especially those near the Playhouse. I feared knocking someone over at every turn.

The next problem was how to suspend the screen. Those familiar with the Playhouse will be aware of the beams across the building. After much thought, bearing in mind the distance of throw from projector to screen, it was decided it must be suspended between the first two beams in front of the old cinema screen. Some bright spark suggested hanging it from 'sky-hooks'!! A better suggestion came with the construction of an 'H' section between the beams. With measurements taken, timber bought and painted, there then came the job of getting it all up there. After a long struggle, most of it was up, but a volunteer was required to secure a couple of points. The committee members present volunteered Adrian for this task, after all, he looked the lightest ( and bravest ). We all held the ladder — we had to, nothing could be secured till Adrian knocked home a few well placed 6'' nails. Back on the ground, Adrian was praised for a job well done, and it was only then, when Adrian mentioned his weight, that we discovered I was almost a stone lighter. I assured him I didn't know as he looked much lighter than I did.

The screen was bolted to a wooden batten, both being raised or lowered to suit our needs and storage. The whole contraption was manoeuvered up or down by clothes lines, which were secured to a conveniently positioned radiator. We never dared to leave the screen suspended, fearing its weight might bring the whole lot crashing down one night onto some poor and unsuspecting bingo player.

Next came the projection end. As all the old cinema equipment had been removed a few years earlier, it was really a case of a good clean and tidy-up, and finding the best position for the projector. We decided to remove one of the plate glass projection portholes, thus allowing better transmission of light, and hopefully resulting in a brighter picture. In total ignorance, Adrian set to work attacking the plate glass with a hammer, while I collected the glass into a sack. After much effort, the job was well done. ( It was many years later we discovered the glass and frame would have come out more easily by just unscrewing four wing-nuts! ).

The next mammoth task was feeding a loudspeaker cable from the projection box to a loudspeaker sited near the screen. This proved messy, as we had to try to conceal our cable from sight.

Membership was growing at a steady pace. By mid-June we had over 70 paid up members, and they were coming in daily. This boosted our confidence immensely.

We still had many things yet to organise before our first night, and as our membership increased we felt we must cover up the prize bingo equipment and prizes, not only in the interest of security, but to make the whole place look like a cinema again. The solution was the purchase of a large black polythene sheet 21 feet wide by 8 feet deep, which would have to be pinned into supporting battens for each show. The polythene sheet was effectively used for almost a year until our purchase of a curtain we could raise and lower, thus making the screen end more attractive.

Once the season's films were confirmed by the distributors and our credit worthiness assessed, we were able to announce our selection of films. We prepared a simple newsletter and programme combined, briefly explaining that as we only had one projector this would necessitate reel changes at the end of every reel, approximately every forty minutes.

The first film arrived over a week early, giving me ample opportunity to check and clean it in preparation for the big night. On the Sunday before our Monday opening, Adrian transported the projector etc.down to the Playhouse and set it up.[14] After the bingo finished, all the committee came down to prepare for the Monday show. Small card tables and chairs had to be disposed of, bingo and related signs removed, the screen fitted to the batten and positioned. Our black polythene sheet needed fitting and many more small jobs were necessary to get the place looking right. This Sunday night preparation was just another job that continued throughout the years, although with a few improvements along the way it was made considerably easier.

At last it arrived — our opening night, and 'our' gala performance of the Academy Award-winning film, 'Tom Jones' starring Albert Finney and Susannah York, and what a night for excitement. Even though I retired to the projection box for my projectionist duties, I could feel the tremendous atmosphere throughout the cinema. My ambition of seeing films back again at the Playhouse was fulfilled, and it was — dare I say — my 'own cinema'. Our first night audience totalled 124 including guests, and from a total membership of 162 we were more than pleased with the results of our labours. But our work didn't finish when the members left, for we had to clean up (we couldn't afford to pay a cleaner) and revert everything back for the following night's bingo session. We were so pleased with our first few shows that we decided to add an extra film, Julie Andrews in 'Star' ( 1968, Dir: Robert Wise) bringing our first season's total up to nine.

As I mentioned earlier, most of our films were arriving a week before the playdate, giving me sufficient time to clean, check, and repair any damage. However, over the years we did encounter a few problems with deliveries. The first occurred with the seventh film in our first season, 'Chitty Chitty Bang Bang' ( 1968, Dir: Ken Hughes). The film consisted of five reels in two separate transit cases, but due to a rail strike, we were prepared for a slight delay! Parts four and five arrived on the Saturday prior to the Monday show, but no parts one, two or three. This caused me great worry, fearing a possible cancellation of the show. Numerous phone calls to postal sorting offices in Beverley, Hull and Leeds had drawn blanks. I was at a loss until our local postal sorting office telephoned — we could have our show. The missing reels arrived at 11.00 a.m. on the show day and our programme was complete. [15]

---

[14] This transportation of equipment continued for quite some time until we managed to purchase our own projector. [15] The problems of film arriving on time, especially during the high demand season October to March, often meant films arriving far too close for comfort to our Monday playdates. So, after lengthy and favourable negotiations with Columbia-EMI-Warner Ltd., we were able to have the loan of a standby film of our choice from their list for the cost of postage in both directions only. Eventually, the postal and rail services were to be replaced by Securicor deliveries and collections. Even so, film arrivals in the busy season often caused concern. Thankfully, favourable negotiatons with the Rank film library secured an early despatch date for all of their programmes.

Another problem arose with our following show, 'The Most Dangerous Man In The World' (1969, Dir: J. Lee Thompson). It wasn't a print delivery problem this time, but something equally serious as you will see. The main film was a bit on the short side, and even with the supporting film the programme was still short. So, I decided that as Christmas was only weeks away I would attempt to be safety conscious and show an additional supporting film on fire prevention. Having seen a very suitable one belonging to the local fire prevention department, I contacted them and they jumped at the idea. On the night of the show, the fire officer brought his film and was invited to stay on for the full programme. The main film had just started when looking out into the auditorium from the projection box I spotted a lady walking out into the foyer. Seconds later she returned. Adrian, by this time, had approached and attended to her. Thinking it was someone who didn't like the look of the film and had left, I thought no more of the matter. The following morning, I received a phone call from a very serious-sounding fire prevention officer wanting to know why the front door of the Playhouse had been locked or bolted, thus preventing the exit of the members. A sudden sinking feeling hit my stomach. Could this mean closure? To my knowledge no doors had been locked or bolted. Adrian was the theatre manager, and I had total confidence in his understanding of the safety regulations. The fire officer requested that we both meet him at the Playhouse at twelve noon. I managed to get hold of Adrian, and he assured me no doors had been locked or bolted. This he confirmed when we met at the cinema. This is when we discovered fully what had happened. An elderly lady, (Member No. 147) had decided to leave the show. She couldn't find her way out of a side exit, was unable to push the front door open, so the next day she had phoned our chairman to complain. Unable to get him she phoned the fire department stating that she had been locked in the Playhouse with over 200 people. Thankfully, with the fire officer present at the show he knew the audience size she quoted was an exaggeration (in fact it was 107 including one fire officer). We were let off, and although all the doors had been unlocked, this one incident was to lead us all to becoming more aware of our responsibility to our members and guests.

As our existing members started renewing their subscriptions for the second season, we soon discovered there were many more who wanted to join. With the existing set up we could not accommodate the numbers we anticipated, so we started thinking about using the old cinema screen. Its use would mean all seats could be used. Mrs. Symmons wasn't too keen on the idea as it meant considerable disruption to the prize bingo display shelves and other equipment. So, in an effort to help us get a larger and better screen, she kindly offered to meet us half way with the cost of a new one. Without delay, we found a suitably priced 12 by 10 feet roller screen that could be neatly rolled up in its box out of sight and dust. [16]

Our first season ended with 'From Russia With Love'. Our total attendance of members and guests reached 1,067, an average of 118 per show. Membership increased rapidly, as did our enthusiasm. Our next season would open with our big new screen. Sadly, we still had only one projector, but no-one appeared to mind the reel changes. In fact, some actually welcomed them. We did eventually manage to purchase our own projector, but it was to be a few years before we could afford two projectors and run a continuous programme.

Over the Christmas holiday and into the new year of 1973, I decided to have a root (with permission) through some of the drawers in the office where I knew there was a 'treasure chest' of old papers and a scrap book. I thought it was about time I started researching the history of the Playhouse and Ernest Symmons.

I became totally absorbed in my findings, many of which have helped to formulate this book.

As I discovered details of some of the films Ernest had made I became saddened at our hand in the disposal and destruction of many thousands of feet of film, but the decision to dispose had been made for us by the fire department. I am afraid I do not know the circumstances surrounding the initial move, but as bingo halls came under close scrutiny by the fire department, the discovery of numerous cans of the very unstable and combustable nitrate film caused great concern for the safety of the Playhouse and surrounding property.

In the mass clear out, film was found stored near heating pipes under the balconies, and in almost every free space in the building. Upon realising the quantity of film (I estimated in the region of 33,000 feet) the need to dispose became urgent. Mrs. Symmons, her step-daughter and some of the staff — myself included — spent the best part of a week sorting the films out and ensuring they were packed into cans and transit cases to pass on to the smelting company for silver recovery. I remember opening one can of film and watching it literally disintegrate before my eyes. It is a great loss that none of the films could have been saved and preserved properly until such time as a safe copy could be made, but this was impossible, mainly due to poor storage over the years.

As an indication of the cost of copying old films, in June 1984 I contacted the National Film Archive with a view to purchasing a copy of one of the

[16] Even the new and bigger screen posed problems. Three eight-foot fluorescent tubes hung on chains, previously not in the way, now obstructed the projection beam. The solution — messy but effective — meant a series of pulleys being fitted to the high roof beams and extra long lengths of clothes lines through them to the light fittings. The other ends were concealed as much as possible down the walls. So, for show nights we hoisted the lights out of the way. It was crude and unsightly, but it worked. However, gradually and over a period of weeks we shortened the chains, hoping that neither Mrs. S. nor anyone else would notice. Eventually our problem was no longer.

first films shown at the Playhouse on opening night in 1911. My intention had been to show this film at a future Film Festival but at a cost of about £150 plus vat for only 211 feet of 16mm, with a running time of just over seven minutes, I was forced to abandon the idea.

We hadn't even screened the first film of our second season in 1973 before both film society and social club received a broadside leaving us to recoil in shock and panic. A small healine appeared in the January 4th issue of the Hull 'Daily Mail', announcing, 'Plans for Playhouse and Baths'. The plans were to convert the Playhouse into shop units, and the Baths into a multi-functional hall. This press announcement was the first we knew of any proposed developments. Mrs. Symmons had made an application for a renewal of the lease for five years, but according to the press, this had, subject to planning approval, been turned down by the planning committee.

I phoned one person who I thought could possibly help us, Richard Wilson. (Richard was at that time a lecturer in English Literature at York University). His concern for the Playhouse's future was reflected in immediate action on his part and advice to us.

Four days after the first announcement of the plans for the cinema site came the healine from the Hull 'Daily Mail' on January 8th: 'The Beverley plea for Playhouse to stay as a Cinema'. This was the result of Richard Wilson's prompt action in writing to the Town Clerk, Mr. Roy Gregory. Richard asked what consideration had been given to the idea of retaining the Playhouse as a cinema, particularly at a time when the newly-formed film society was gaining greater support. In describing the Playhouse, Richard referred to it as 'a remarkable piece of cinema architecture' and a 'slice of social history which need not have outlived its usefulness'.

On Richard's advice we were all encouraged to write letters of objection to the development proposals. This we did. On Tuesday, January 9th, the Hull 'Daily Mail' headline carried happier news, 'Reprieve for Beverley Playhouse'. The whole development matter had been referred back for further consideration. Our reprieve was only temporary, but at least it provided a breathing space.

We all felt it was only a matter of time before the next attack, so a petition was launched. I brought our plight to the attention of the Yorkshire Arts Association, The Cinema Theatre Association and anyone else with the remotest interest in us and our activities. I was impressed with the letter from the Yorkshire Arts Association to the Council that our film society 'the youngest in Yorkshire, is undoubtedly one of the best', and definitely worth fighting for.

In February, the Town Clerk, on behalf of the Council, cleared the air over the Playhouse plans by saying that due to a misunderstanding over the future use of the Playhouse, they had no intentions of demolishing the building, but due to the old public baths closing, and the Playhouse lease expiring, the Council decided 'to consider how the buildings could best benefit the town'. In the meantime the Council had decided to permit the tenants of the Playhouse to remain there for a further year.

Even with a year's reprieve we had little confidence in a secure future. We dare not rest. Our petition had collected 2,153 signatures and was presented to the Borough Council for their deliberation.

Around this time television played a major role in our campaign, when the B.B.C. 'Look North' team became aware of our plight. They saw this sad story as a potential news item. The outcome was a ten minute documentary introduced by Philip Hayton outlining the Playhouse history and some of the people behind it, including clips from some of Ernest's films. Emphasis was also made on the situation surrounding the threatened re-development plans.

On February 16th, the 'Beverley Guardian' announced 'Playhouse reprieved for 13 months', but almost a week later, on February 22nd, the 'Daily Mail' carried a headline 'Council asked to push on with Playhouse shops'! The Beverley Corporation Highways and Planning Committee, asked the Town Council to proceed with preparation of detailed plans to convert the Playhouse into shops.

As the public baths next door to the Playhouse would become extinct when the new baths opened, a suggestion came for the conversion of the old baths to a multi-functional hall, which could be used as a theatre, dance hall, social centre and provide a transfer of our social and film activities from the Playhouse. This idea was totally impractical from the point of its restrictive size, and the need for blackout and acoustic treatments. This may have made it unsuitable for other uses, and without fixed seats we, the film society committee, could envisage similar problems to those of the ill-fated Memorial Hall.

An assurance came from the Chairman of the Corporation Highways and Planning committee, Councillor Albert Meadley. He said, 'Both television and the press have implied that the Playhouse would be knocked down and replaced by shops. This has never been our intention'.

Besides the shop idea, the Council also had inquiries from other parties interested in converting the Playhouse into a night club, licensed restaurant, office accommodation, craft centre and supermarket, but thankfully, we had many friends and followers who wanted to see us continue operating as a social club and 'cinema club'.

One of our friends, Alderman Harry Flynn, felt it was a final chance of preserving a cinema service in Beverley, and described the Playhouse as the last bastion of cinema-going in the area.

In April 1973 came another surprise, as the question was asked: 'Could Council run Playhouse?' This idea was based on the municipally run cinema by Penistone Urban Council, in the West Riding, and although it ran at a small loss, proved to be a valuable amenity to the town. The idea of a Council run cinema disappeared without a trace. After all, the

Corporation owned Memorial Hall Cinema, running once a fortnight, had only lasted a few months.

Throughout these times of uncertainty, both the social club and film society bravely continued, giving the outward impression of security. We all tried hard not to reveal our fears for the future.

In early June, Mrs. Symmons published a twelve page report entitled 'A study of the Property known as the Picture Playhouse and Corporation Swimming Baths'. This was a very impressive and detailed study of these properties, and had involved a considerable amount of work, not just by Mrs. Symmons but by her stepson Brenton Symmons, two senior social club staff and myself. Over eighty copies of this report were sent or delivered to members of the Council, and everyone with our interests at heart. The actual presentation of the report was of a high standard, each one being accompanied by a letter from Mrs. Symmons and presented in a plastic wallet, that I felt proud delivering this excellent work. I am confident in thinking that as a result of this report, our efforts were rewarded with a further extension to the lease, thus allowing us to continue operations until March 31st, 1975.

During this time of insecurity, the film society was unable to expand the facilities as it would have liked. We dare not apply for any of the financial grants available to us when our closure could come at the end of the reprieve period.

Early in 1973 the film society began planning a film festival. Our aim was to present as many of Ernest's surviving films as possible in an evening of nostalgia, the proceeds being donated to local charities. The show was a sell out, with numerous requests for a repeat show. This was easier said than done. Our first 'Symmons Film Festival' had taken just over eight months to prepare. A friend, Peter Richardson, had done so much research on the availability of suitable films and provided many to make up the programme, while Jack and May Lawson devised and compiled appropriate soundtracks. (Here I would add that this team was to be responsible for our success with two more charity film festivals in 1977 and 1980). [17]

As we entered 1974, our film society funds were sufficient enough for us to purchase our own projector, and along with mine we now had two machines. We still could not run a continuous show however, as our funds would not stretch to buying a second matched zoom lens, or provide 'change over' facilities.

Consideration was given to a long play unit, which would have allowed us on many occasions to run the whole programme without a break, but we had to consider the time taken in making up the programme onto large reels. That idea was scrapped, but with our new projector we now had the luxury of automatic threading. This reduced our reel change time on most occasions to approximately one minute.

[17] Sadly, any further festivals will have to be without Peter's expertise and help as he died in December 1984 during the final stages of this book's production.

Reel changes were to continue for another two seasons until in 1975 we received a donation of £508 from the defunct Hull and District Film Society. The money enabled us to purchase a second projector, matched zoom lens and change over unit, plus necessary modifications to the projection box.

1975 brought again that sickly feeling that closure could be near. The committee had frequently discussed plans for the worst happening, should a lease renewal fail. In fact, so confident were we that this would be it, we advised all our members of our anticipated end.

As the time grew nearer, Mrs. Symmons and I made numerous visits to our solicitor, who negotiated the lease, and again we won a reprieve — this time not a year, but three whole years, to expire in 1978. The lease this time had strings attached. Firstly, the Council wanted more rent. Mrs. Symmons offered to meet them halfway in their demands. Secondly, the front of the Playhouse had to be tidied up, at the recommendation by members of the Civic Society. This involved the removal of light fittings, repairs to roof, pointing of the brickwork, reduction in the size of poster display boards, and a re-paint, and as scaffolding had to be used it proved to be a costly business which rate payers believed to be at their expense. Mrs. Symmons was quick to reassure them through a letter in the 'Beverley Guardian' that it was she and not they who would be footing the bill.

Feeling secure at the Playhouse, for three years at least, I started thinking about the possible expansion of the film facilities. My plan was to open the Playhouse one night a week as a commercial 16mm cinema. This, I anticipated, could run alongside the bingo and film society. I applied for and was granted a license. I needed about £2,000 to upgrade the equipment, but the bank had little interest in the venture and declined their support. However, once the press got hold of the story most of my financial worries practically disappeared with offers of cash, help and investments from several friends and some businessmen in the town.

Initially, most of the film distributors were very helpful, as were the advertising agencies, until they realised that the screenings were to be for only a single night. This put a new and expensive light on the situation. The distributors said they would have to charge a much higher rental for their products as one night per week was not financially viable. I could see their point, and so ended another chapter in my attempts to run a cinema.

The film society continued to attract a healthy membership, and by mid-1977 membership had reached 317, over double the opening target I had set five years earlier in 1972. The subscription had been increased by a mere 50p over this period, bringing it up to only £2.00. [18]

[18] The reader may be interested to know that each time we held a film festival our membership increased for that particular season. This I feel was the result of the publicity surrounding each one, and my frequent press appeals for any old films made by Ernest that could possibly be included in a festival. These requests never failed to generate an interest in our activities.

In 1978, we gave our members a special treat with a show aimed specially for the youngsters. This was the 'Mickey Mouse Anniversary Show' (1971, Dir: Ward Kimball), and as a result we received favourable comments from the British Federation of Film Societies in their magazine 'Film'. They referred to us as being 'Enterprising' and as one of the earliest 'Community Cinemas'. Here was praise indeed, especially as our commercial programming policy had come under close scrutiny and criticism so many times before.

Another event worthy of celebration in the same year was a further two year extension to the lease, but the reduction of a year on the last lease once again hinted the degree of uncertainty we had come so often to expect. However, around this time we were having problems with our glass roof. Light and rain had begun to sneak in, water ran down walls and dripped in all over the place. Our biggest worry was keeping the electrical installations dry, especially those used for bingo and emergency lights; so when the rains came so did the buckets, ashtrays and any other suitable receptacles.

These problems were eventually solved when Mrs. Symmons decided to have a new roof constructed over the glass one, for which the cost was well over £2,000. Consideration was given to the total removal of the glass, but the additional cost of glass removal and plastering the area (45′ × 15″ approx.) was to cost half as much again as the roof. So, it was decided that as the glass had now ceased to be a problem it would stay in situ.

1979 saw the introduction of the film society's first newsletter. This provided us with an ideal vehicle for better communication with our members. This was also the year of experiments. The first was the addition of sound effects with rumbles accompanying the film 'Earthquake' (1974, Dir: Mark Robson). Originally, the film was presented in certain cinemas with 'Sensurround'. This was a system using high-intensity, low frequency sounds, thus enabling one to 'feel' as well as hear the sound of earthquakes, explosions and the like. For our one night show a series of earthquake rumbles were recorded onto a tape cassette.

The cassette tape was then fed through our stereo system minus treble, but with maximum bass and Dolby into the auditorium via five speakers, while the soundtrack was reproduced through twelve speakers. The rumbles, crashes etc., were operated manually, and introduced at the appropriate moments throughout the film, and from the audience's view point proved quite effective.

At the end of March, we had for the first time in Beverley, a screening of 'The Ten Best' amateur films of 1978. These were the ten winning films from the 'Movie Maker' magazine annual amateur film competition. Sadly, only 83 people came to the show. In contrast to 'The Ten Best' a more successful show was presented bringing another 'first' with the 3D presentation of 'The Creature from the Black Lagoon' (1954, Dir: Jack

Arnold). This attracted an audience of 233, and although the 3D system used was 'anaglyphic' (the red and green system as opposed to the polaroid), the audience reaction was very favourable, encouraging us to consider a further 3D presentation.

Our pre-Christmas film brought a novel and uninvited 'special effect' producing many chuckles. The film was Walt Disney's 'The Island at the Top of the World' (1974, Dir: Robert Stevenson), and told of the adventures of a band of explorers on their balloon trip to the top of the world.

On this night, celebrations had taken place at the switching on of the Christmas lights at the other end of town, the children being given gas-filled balloons. One child brought his balloon to the Playhouse and let it go, up to the cciling it floated, and stayed, leaving one very sad child. However, with the excitement of the film it was soon forgotten, until about two thirds of the way through the film, for this was when the green balloon started a slow descent, a matter of inches in front of the screen, much to the amusement of the audience. Our year had started with planned effects, and endcd with an unplanned one.

For some time we had given serious thought to and discussed the possibilities of screening CinemaScope films at the society shows. About 50% of the films available to us were in Scope, as well as standard ratio, a few good titles being available in Scope only. To show both would definitely make our presentations more professional. However, there were snags. We managed to buy a pair of Anamorphic lenses quite reasonably which was a start. At least we could unsqueeze the picture, but the main problem was a screen. Once again, we contemplated using the old cinema screen, but due to its poor condition, along with the bingo equipment being in the way, we had to again abandon the idea.

The only solution would be to buy a new screen. Realising this could be costly, we started thinking about fund-raising. Various ideas were put forward, including those of a lottery, coffee mornings and jumble sales. These were abandoned in favour of our receiving a third of the total proceeds from the 1980 Symmons film festival, the other two thirds being donated to local charities. Of course, we were still unsure about our future. The lease was due to expire during the course of this year and we didn't know if we would be granted a further extension. The news of the lease came in November, when, on November 19th, the 'Daily Mail' announced 'Beverley Cinema Saved'.

The Playhouse site would not be developed for five years, and the Council also agreed to extend the lease until May 31st, 1981. However, the lease holders of both the Playhouse and the old public baths, our next door neighbours (Sellit and Soon), were given the option of renewing for a further five years.

With news like that our future was definitely secure for many more seasons to come. This urged us to look more seriously into the installation of Scope. Various tests were carried out, and after deliberation it was decided that our number one priority was to increase our light output before we could present satisfactory and acceptable pictures in Scope. So, for the time being, we would concentrate on upgrading the projection end rather than the screen end, and the only way to do this would be to sell our two projectors etc., and purchase a single projector with long play facilities and a powerful Xenon lamp. This would give us a much brighter picture and help us in our eventual aim for satisfactory CinemaScope, but our hold up was again to be insufficient funds.

Early in 1981, our funds received a boost as the result of our hosting a special public show for some of the local driving schools. The event was planned and organised by Adrian Moore a founder member of the society's original committee, and himself a driving instructor. The show was a huge success, with an audience of almost 300. Expenses paid, a residue of £100 remained, so the organisers donated £40 to our funds and £60 to the equipment funds of the Westwood Hospital, Beverley.

As the film society's popularity continued, we looked to the future and the hope that one day soon we would have that new screen and projector, thus giving our members the very best that 16mm presentation could offer.

However, on the social club side of the Playhouse, bingo attendances had fallen to an average of between two and three hundred a week, while our society shows were attracting this size of audience for practically every show.

I became saddened and depressed to see the once very popular Friday night bingo audiences fall to less than one hundred, except for when the jackpot of snowball numbers were high, then we could probably reach an attendance of 120! But our Saturdays were worse still. One July Saturday I noted in my diary that it had been a 'terrible night, only 18 in, worst I think I have ever known'. But one wet, windy September night it was even worse when only 14 bravely ventured out to play bingo. As a bingo caller calling to such small audiences I soon began to loose heart in the job. With so few people playing, the games would last for ages and the prize money became so pathetically small. As a result, on many occasions additional money was added by Mrs. Symmons to make the winnings just a bit more interesting. Certainly our hard cord regulars appreciated this for they stuck with us through good and bad. I seriously began to wonder just how long we could continue since we must by now be losing money.

After much thought, Mrs. Symmons decided that we must make an attempt to halt the flow of bingo players leaving the Playhouse in favour of the Regal, so, we offered the biggest jackpot ever — £1,000. [19] This was the big one.

It *had* to attract some of our members back from the opposition. We

[19] The first £1,000 jackpot was won on a Sunday night that had attracted only 49 players.

circulated our members with full details of our 'exciting new bingo', offering '25 chances to win' each night, and free admission. This was the one thing I was not too happy about.

Free admission had been done before at the Marble Arch, and had failed. Our only income from bingo would then come from a participation fee of 5p on each book sold, the fruit machines and colour bingo, which would not represent much on poorer nights.

I have to admit that although I was enthusiastic about our new venture I had serious misgivings about its success. In my opinion, we had let our business slip, while the opposition watched and studied our every move with care and caution, benefiting all the time from our mistakes.

In early August it was decided that we should close on Saturday nights, but our Saturday regulars became quite upset, for, after all, this was the only night they had a chance to play for the £1,000 jackpot. So, after three Saturdays of closure we re-opened again, but only for two weeks, for after that wet September Saturday and our 'grand' attendance of 14, the decision was final that that was the last Saturday night we would be open.

# CHAPTER SEVEN

**The End?**

On September 29th, 1981, I received news I had expected for some time. Mrs. Symmons phoned in confidence to say she expected to close the Playhouse on January 6th, 1982. On Friday, October 16th, I announced to our bingo players that we would be closing at the end of that night's session. There was uproar against this decision. With many pleas for us to remain open, the loyalty from our members was appreciated; but due to lack of support as a result of declining interest and many of our members playing their game at the Regal, we had no alternative but to close. However, a temporary compromise was reached, we would remain open for two nights a week, Tuesday and Friday, until December 22nd.

On the film society side we had discussed the possibility of alternative premises to continue the shows, but nothing would have compared with the convenience and comfort the Playhouse afforded, so we too took the decision to cease our operations on the night of our last show of the season, December 7th. Our members were advised of our closure, and those who had paid subscriptions for our 20th season, the first season of 1982, were guaranteed a full refund.

As we prepared to close, a glimmer of hope for a continuation of films in Beverley came from a timber importer and his wife, Jon and Pat Gresham. I had known them both for quite a few years, ever since they had expressed an interest in the Playhouse as a possible venue for the display of their marvellous collection of coin operated and mechanical amusement machines. However, they had acquired the Ritz Cinema at Pocklington for this purpose, eventually converting the former stalls into the very impressive Penny Arcadia, and retaining a 250 seat cinema on the balcony.

On hearing of our closure, Jon and Pat Gresham were very keen on the possibility of acquiring the lease when Mrs. Symmons finished, with a view to re-opening the Playhouse as a cinema again. Cinema interest also came from two other people; one a cinema enthusiast who would have liked to share the building with bingo for so many nights a week; the second was a property development company, who I believe saw the Playhouse not just as a cinema operation, but looked to possible future developments.

On November 17th, the Beverley Borough Council agreed to negotiate a deal with Crownbridge Ltd. This was of course Jon and Pat's company. So, subject to satisfactory negotiations and a licence being granted, the cinema would be re-opening early in 1982. Jon and Pat made repeated requests for me to manage their cinema for them, but I was very tired and I wanted a rest from the Playhouse. My sole aim was to just go and see a film each week and not be involved.

In no time at all, December 7th and the last society show arrived. The last film, our 244th, was 'The Lord of the Rings' (1979, Dir: Ralph Bakshi) and was attended by 162 members and guests, bringing our grand attendance record since our opening on July 17th, 1972, to 44,274. Before the show started, the committee and members paid tribute to my years of service to the society by presenting me with eight Royal Doulton porcelain figures of characters from the film 'Lord of the Rings'.

Although the society activities had come to an end on December 9th, the Playhouse was used for a public meeting and film show, after which the equipment was dismantled and the screen taken down for transportation to Alloa in Scotland, where a small town hall cinema waited for their bigger screen.

The projection and allied equipment was sold, the proceeds being added to the central fund, which, after all expenses had been paid, was distributed to film societies, an amateur theatre group, and numerous charitable organisations. In total these donations and amounts raised as a result of film festivals etc., had enabled the society to have donated over £3,000 to various worthwhile causes over its 9½ years of operations.

I feel the Playhouse Film Society's activities were best summed up by David Watterson, General Secretary of the British Federation of Film Societies, in his letter to us at the end of our operations: 'We have not always seen eye to eye on programming, but the sheer effort, determination and ingenuity of the Playhouse Film Society has been a constant example to us all'.

December 22nd, brought bingo finally to an end at the Playhouse. Sadly, I thought that after all the years of social club activities the place would have been packed on the last night with many old members coming just for old times sake, but a mere 117 came to say goodbye, and so ended another chapter in the history of the Picture Playhouse.

# CHAPTER EIGHT

## A New Beginning

The job of clearing out all the bingo equipment now commenced. By January 6th, 1982 the date the lease expired, practically all traces of bingo had gone, leaving the place almost looking as it had done in pre-bingo days. I was asked to keep an eye on the building until such times as a fair decision was made over Jon Gresham taking over the Playhouse as a cinema. I did not enjoy going in during this transition period. Everything was so uninteresting, although I was not the only one to visit the Playhouse, for I discovered on one occasion that the exit lights had been left on, and the torches the film society had left had gone as had the coffee!!

A phone call on January 26th from Jon Gresham confirmed his acquisition of the Playhouse lease for four years commencing February 15th. This was wonderful news, for it meant cinema would return to Beverley. Again I was requested to manage the Playhouse, but didn't feel I could face the prospect. Nevertheless, after much persuasion, I accepted.

The job of getting the Playhouse up to scratch for a cinema again began with great enthusiasm. This involved the complete clearance of the area behind the old screen to accommodate a corridor through which the new patrons could enter from the opposite side, thus reducing stray light and draughts entering the auditorium. The old sound equipment (and much dust) was moved to make way for the new loudspeakers.

A number of newer and slightly more comfortable seats were 'imported' from the Pocklington cinema. These were destined to replace many of the old seats on the balconies. Four rows of existing seats were taken up in the back stalls, and re-laid as three rows, greatly increasing the leg room. Next came the front stalls. The removal of the bingo equipment had left an enormous space at the front, so to help fill this gap and as an aid to improving the space between each row, all but two rows of the front stall seats were taken up and re-laid, again allowing more leg room. This work alone occupied three colleagues and myself at weekends and evenings for the best part of a month.

The projection equipment arrived and was installed. It looked good to see a 35mm projector at the Playhouse again. [20]

[20] This was a KALEE 19 with a BTH arc converted to a Xenon lamp. The use of one projector means that all films have to be made up onto large spools of 12000 feet capacity, thus enabling the continuous projection of a feature film lasting just over two hours. The film is supplied from and taken up by a separate motorised unit standing at the side of the projector.

An opening date of Monday, April 5th had been planned. The first film was to be the twentieth animated feature film from the Disney studio, 'The Fox and the Hound' (1981). After careful inspection of the old screen, it was considered too badly stained to be usable, so on April 2nd a new screen was installed. The side drapes had all been washed, re-hung and fire proofed. The seats and carpets had been vacuumed, and, after weeks of upheaval the Playhouse was now looking ready for opening. A carefully picked and trained staff eagerly and nervously awaited opening night.

Opening night finally arrived, and although I wasn't officially working that night, I had to be there. This was the moment for which I had waited for fourteen years — the return of a commercial cinema to Beverley. An excited audience of 142, mainly comprised of children, brought life back to the Playhouse with their excitement. I was nervous: Would anything go wrong? Would it be a success? Whatever happened, nothing could spoil the enjoymemt of this first evening and the excitement I felt. I had come a bit closer to that ambition of owning a cinema. Films had returned on a full-time basis to the town, but more importantly to the Playhouse, and I was the Manager.

During the first few months of operation, I found young children and teenagers could be a nuisance by chattering and often walking about. This worried me as it would distract the more mature cinemagoers. The problem was, I felt, caused by television. Many of them had never been to a cinema, so sitting and watching a 'big telly' was in some respects like watching TV at home, where it is easier to chat and go for a little walk during commercials. Some of the younger children have actually found the big picture a bit overwhelming, and have on occasions been reduced to tears.

The story of the Playhouse does not end yet, for we have had a few hiccups along the way. Two rectifiers have failed on us. These convert the AC electricity into DC required for running the Xenon lamp. The original film take-up system developed a very loud and embarrassing groan that could be heard in the rear stalls. However, this was, after my persistent nattering, replaced in 1984 with a Westrex 5035 Film Carrier Assembly. [21]

We had problems with our 'Scope' picture (have you heard that before?). The first anamorphic lens appeared to lose too much light. The second one, although much better, was only loaned to us for a short time. The third and current one, the Dyaliscope, is my own, and is one of the pair originally installed in November 1962 in an attempt to improve the presentation of 'Ben Hur'.

[21] The film carrier assembly, also known as a 'Tower Unit' is a large box-like construction standing over six feet high by about two feet square. It carries on each of two opposite sides a pair of 13000-foot spool positions each pair arranged one spool above the other. The whole unit is mounted on a turntable so that at the end of a programme the machine can be rotated through 180° to bring the next pair of spools into line with the projector's film path and the new film threaded with a minimum of delay. Whilst one pair is in use for the programme the other pair can be used for rewinding, or for make up and break down of a programme.

Towards the end of 1982, I began to notice a steady stream of regular cinemagoers who reminded me a bit of the regular bingo players. One group in particular have supported us on Sunday nights almost from the beginning: Our friends the 'bikers'. At first, I will admit, I feared their presence, arriving in their leathers. I didn't know what to expect. My thoughts had flashed to the gang in the film 'Mad Max'!! but how wrong I was. I was soon to learn never to judge people by the clothes they wear, for my biker friends are some of our best and most regular cinemagoers.

The many children of Beverley have become regular cinemagoers, not just to our evening performances (when suitable), but our Saturday afternoon specials. These children's matinees are, in essence, similar to the ABC minors' matinees I attended as a child, but there the similarity ends, for we have endeavoured to encourage the children into taking as much an active part as possible in addition to the films, which, incidentally, are specially made or compiled by the Children's Film Foundation. We have introduced four teams, each represented by a leader, who, as well as assisting with the supervision and safety of the children, are encouraged to participate in games and activities to represent their respective teams. The winning team to receive the highest number of points is awarded the Michael Philips trophy. [22] This takes place every seven weeks.

Points are awarded to the children for team activities as well as individual efforts, like bringing paintings or helping clear up etc. Many parents have expressed appreciation for our care and patience with their children. Anyone will soon realise the immense amount of work in keeping a constant watch on a number of children, especially in the dark, but I feel the staff do derive a lot of pleasure from the matinee kids. It does have its rewards, like the home-made sweets we had brought covered in fingerprints and wrapped in something vaguely resembling toilet paper; or the numerous sweets usually unwrapped which are offered from a grubby hand or dusted with fluff.

To us, a Saturday matinee means confiscating itching powder, spending ten minutes searching the floor with a torch for a penny, comforting a frightened child while his nose runs on your shirt, rescuing the little ones who couldn't get out of the toilet, comforting and curing a bleeding nose and many more activities too numerous to list. These are the little things that make a matinee, but the most important ingredient is staff who can deal with these situations, and not only laugh afterwards but come each week for more. One member of our staff has made more than an effort to make the matinees the success they are. I feel I must, as my history of the Playhouse comes towards its end, mention Robert Curry, for he, as Master of Ceremonies, has won the favour and trust of our little ones.

Robert has been our key to success. My next ambition is to see these children coming to the Playhouse in their teens and twenties, with

[22] Kindly donated by a local jeweller of the same name.

boyfriends and girlfriends — for I am confident they will be the perfect cinemagoers. That is, of course, if any cinemas are left for them.

As I mentioned much earlier in this book, music has played an important part at the Playhouse over the years. In 1983 we hosted Beverley's first folk festival, an event I did not look forward to, especially as a stage and bar had to be erected. I had no idea what sort of people would be attracted, nor what mess or damage could be expected. My worries were needless. The people were fantastic, mess and damage nil.

In 1984 we hosted Beverley's second Folk Festival. This time I welcomed the audience with open arms. In the two festivals, well over 2,000 people came to the concerts to experience a feast of entertainment, and many have been tremendously enthusiastic about the cinema and its wonderful acoustics.

Unfortunately, my writings are coming to an end. I have tried to cover the years of leisure entertainment and service to the community the Playhouse has given to so many but what of the future? Will we get a wider screen, Stereophonic sound? I think not. What I am sure of is that there is a need for cinema, just as there is a need for TV and video, but which will survive? Dark winter nights are traditional times for cinemagoers, but is any cinema comfortable, warm and attractive enough to lure people away from the new home cinema called video? It's now so easy, as I have discovered, for youngsters under the age of fifteen and eighteen to obtain film I cannot admit them to see, so we lose, where the video dealer wins. Like me, he too is a purveyor of motion picture entertainment, but is not shackled by the strict codes of censorship to which we are subject.

Nevertheless, thanks to films like 'E.T.' (The Extra Terrestrial, 1982, Dir: Steven Spielberg), 'Raiders of the Lost Ark' (1981, Dir: Steven Spielberg), 'Porky's' (1981, Dir: Bob Clark), 'Snow White', 'Jungle Book' and the 'Star Wars' trilogy (1977/79/83, Dir: George Lucas, Irvin Kershner, Richard Marquand), plus a few others, we can still enjoy the pleasure of a full house. I hope that after having read this far you have found something of interest within these pages, and if you think I have omitted anything please forgive me.

In 1986 the Playhouse will be a hundred years old. Let us hope in 2011 we can celebrate a hundred years of entertainment at the Home of Beautiful Pictures.

*Opening frame from the 'Playhouse News'.*

*Soldiers leaving the Playhouse after a screening of the film 'Desert Victory', 1943.*

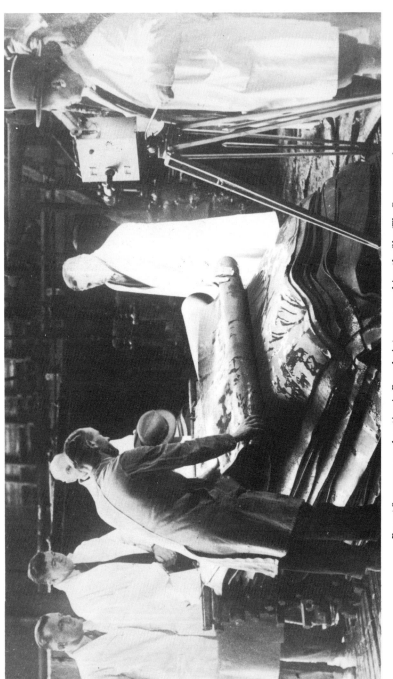

*Ernest Symmons on location in Beverley's tannery making the film 'The Romance of Leather'. It was the first 'talkie' made in Beverley.*

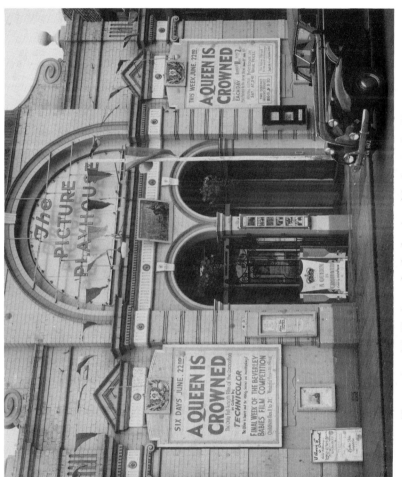

*The exterior of the Playhouse for the showing of the Coronation film, 1953.*

# Sunday Opening.

The Playhouse will be opening once a fortnight starting Sunday (A Man called Peter) Sept. 11th 1955

The doors will be opening approx. 6.40 — Film show starting 7. or 7.15 ending 9.50 or latest 10 oc.

To comply with Regulations — Each Employee working on Sundays (Film Show) will have one full day off the week prior to the Sunday performance — and receive extra pay per rata (4.5 h.p.w) for the three or three half hours work on the Sunday

A log or record of the work done will be kept for the inspection of the Licencing authorities. --

Under no circumstances can an employee be permitted to work or voluntarily give his or her services, at this, or any other theatre, who has been employed for six days the previous week.

*The Notice announcing Sunday opening, September 1955.*

# THE
# PICTURE PLAYHOUSE

### CORN EXCHANGE, BEVERLEY

Proprietress : MRS. THELMA SYMMONS                    'Phone : BEVERLEY 81315

## MAY

| | | |
|---|---|---|
| **THURSDAY, 2nd May** <br> Mat. Sat. 2 p.m. <br> Evenings from 6.15 | *The Last three days of* <br> ## THE 300 SPARTANS <br> *Color by DeLuxe*   (U) | **Richard Egan** <br> **Sir Rph. Richardson** <br> **Diane Baker** |
| **MONDAY, 6th May** <br> Evenings from 6 | *The Rank Organisation presents* <br> ## THE WILD AND THE WILLING <br> *As explosive as youth itself*   (x) | **Virginia Maskell** <br> **Paul Rogers** <br> **Ian McShane** <br> **Samantha Eggar** |
| **THURSDAY, 9th May** <br> Mat. Sat. 2 p.m. <br> Evenings from 6 | *The Rank Organisation prsents* <br> ## BILLY BUDD <br> *MUTINY . . . the word the Navy dreaded most*   (U) | **Robert Ryan** <br> **Peter Ustinov** <br> **Melvyn Douglas** |
| **MONDAY, 13th May** <br> Evenings from 6 | *For Adults only . . . Double Star (x) Programme* <br> ## THE BRIDES OF DRACULA <br> *Technicolor* <br> ## THE THING THAT COULDN'T DIE | **Peter Cushing** <br> **Yvonne Monlaur** <br> **Martita Hunt** <br> **Andre Martin** |
| **THURSDAY, 16th May** <br> Mat. Sat 2 p.m. | *The Rank Organisation presents* <br> ## LIFE FOR RUTH (A) <br> also **BAND OF THIEVES** <br> Starring Mr. Acker Bilk and His Paramount Jazz Band | **Janet Munro** <br> **Michael Craig** <br> **Patrick McGoohan** |
| **MONDAY, 20th May** <br> For three days | *The old and the new—*   *All (U) Programme* <br> ## KNIGHTS OF THE ROUND TABLE <br> ## THE WAR OF THE SATELLITES | **Robert Taylor** |
| **THURSDAY, 23rd May** <br> Mat. Sat. 2 p.m. | *Rider Haggard's* <br> ## KING SOLOMON'S MINES (U) <br> also the Outstanding Western in **LONE STAR** (U) | **Stewart Granger** <br> **Deborah Kerr** <br> **Clark Gable** <br> **Ava Gardner** |
| **MONDAY, 27th May** <br> for SIX DAYS <br> Mat. Sat. 2 p.m. <br> Evenings from 6.15 | *The Rank Organisation presents* <br> ## THE FAST LADY <br> *Technicolor*   (A) <br> *Directed by KEN ANNAKIN    The funniest thing since 'Genevieve'* | **J. R. Justice** <br> **Leslie Phillips** <br> **Stanley Baker** |

## *The Playhouse Bingo and Social Club*
### SUNDAY AFTERNOONS AND NIGHTS
### *Cine-Bingo Monday and Thursday Nights*

*Typical programme of the 1950's.*

*Eyes Down for Bingo.*

**PLAYHOUSE BINGO CLUB - BEVERLEY**

—— Prop.: MRS. T. SYMMONS ——

DEAR MEMBER,

YOU MAY WISH TO KNOW OF OUR EXCITING **NEW** BINGO PROGRAMME WHICH COMMENCES ON **TUESDAY, 18th AUGUST.**

### HERE ARE THE DETAILS

## ADMISSION IS FREE

APPETIZER — 1 GAME — TICKETS 10p EACH
FIVE-TIMER — 10 GAMES — BOOKS 20p EACH
3 x 3 BOOKS — 9 GAMES — BOOKS 15p EACH
BONUS BOOKS — 4 GAMES — BOOKS 15p EACH

—— PLUS ——

### The NEW FEATURE

# £1,000

TICKETS
10p EACH

JACKPOT

ALL BOOKS AND TICKETS INCLUDE A 5p PARTICIPATION FEE

## 25 CHANCES TO WIN

A MEMBER BUYING THREE APPETIZER TICKETS, THREE FIVE-TIMER BOOKS, THREE 3 x 3 BOOKS, THREE BONUS BOOKS AND TWO £1,000 JACKPOT TICKETS HAS A NIGHT OUT FOR ONLY £2.00 AND A CHANCE TO WIN

### THE BIG ONE

HOPE TO SEE YOU SOON.

T. SYMMONS AND STAFF

*The £1,000 Bingo Jackpot.*

*Junior Film Club member, Russell Hayes' impression of E.T. showing at the Playhouse, 1983.*

*The interior (front) of the Playhouse 1985.*

*The interior (rear) of the Playhouse 1985.*

# LIST OF FILMS

This is a list of known films made by the late Mr. Ernest Symmons. In some cases I have been able to find the actual date of production but for many only the month of the year was available. Unfortunately I feel my list is far from complete, however it does present the reader and film historian with a record of very many of the films made by Ernest Symmons.

At the end of this catalogue I have listed a few films of unknown or uncertain dates. As mentioned in the text, some films have survived. Those known to exist I have indicated thus: (S).

**1911**

| | |
|---|---|
| May | Film of Beverley Races (referred to by the press as 'taking notes'). |
| September | Film of York Races, and the St. Ledger at Doncaster |
| October | Employees leaving Messrs. Hodgsons tanyard |
| October | Children leaving school |
| October | Saturday Market during business hours |
| October | Opening stages of Rugby football match Beverley vs Hull |
| October 24 | Ship Launch at Grovehill THE MYNA |
| Oct/Nov | Babies Beauty Contest |
| December 26 | Meet of the Holderness Hounds on Boxing Day |

**1912**

| | |
|---|---|
| January 5 | A new picture of Holderness Hounds at Cherry Burton |
| April | Professor Swizzle F.I.B. |
| April 20 | Launch at Shipyard of Steam trawlers SOLON and PAVLOVA |
| May 30 | Beverley Horse Show |
| November | Babies Beauty Competition (no definite proof of production) |

**1913**

| | |
|---|---|
| January 1 | Holderness Hounds in Beverley Market, views of kennels, Hunting Celebration, Crowds and Motor Cars. |
| January 2 | Wedding of Mr. Billie Hodgson and his bride, Valerie Nelthorpe Palmer. |
| February | Launch at Beverley Shipyard (ship not known) |
| September | St. Ledger |
| September 15 | Local Topical Pictures taken on Westwood |

**1914**

| | | |
|---|---|---|
| January | | Meet of the Holderness Hounds in Market Place (filming not confirmed). |
| March 2 | | Crowds in the Market Place — meet of the Holderness Hounds. |
| June 26 | (S) | Opening of King George Dock, Hull by King George V and Queen Mary. |
| December 16 | (S) | Destruction, after the bombardment of Scarborough, Whitby and Hartlepool. |

**1915**

No record of films made.

**1916**

| | |
|---|---|
| November 5 | Film of Beverley Volunteers [22] ('and the faces of all who took part could be clearly seen'). |
| November 6 | Local Pictures of Mayor's choosing (Mr. Harry Wray) |
| November 13 | Inspection of the Volunteers, [22] the Patriots who do useful work for the country, also the V.C. Hero Pte Chafer. |
| | [22] It is possible that these two films are one and the same. |

# List of films continued

| | |
|---|---|
| November 18 | Unveiling near St. Nicholas Church, Holme Church Lane, Roll of Honour (weather inclement, service held indoors) (no definite confirmation of this film being made). |

## 1917

| | |
|---|---|
| June 16 | Local Film taken of Private Cunningham V.C., and his bride spending the last day of the hero's leave in Beverley. |
| June | Bonniest War Baby competition. |
| August 6 | Beverley Gala and Carnival. |
| September 1 | Wedding of Miss Muriel Wilson at Tranby Croft to Captain Richard Edward Warde, Scots Guards. |

## 1918

| | |
|---|---|
| June 8 | Film of local R.A.F. sports (A number of notable people and celebrities appeared in the film). |

## 1919

| | |
|---|---|
| November 10 | Local Pictures of Mayor's choosing (Councillor and Mrs. David Nutchey). |
| December 26 | Local Film of the meet of the Holderness Hounds on Boxing Day 'Tally Ho' — A two reel film, booked by all the principal halls in the British Isles, and sent to the colonies and America, included a number of runs of the fox and two actual kills including Holderness, York, Ainsty, and Lord Middleton's Hunts, with special hunting music. |

## 1920

| | |
|---|---|
| January | Investiture by H.R.H. Prince Arthur of Connaught of the Royal Scots Greys at York (not confirmed as one of Ernest Symmons' films). |
| March | Modern Dances and how to do them. |

## 1921

Home and Beauty Series — average length 700-800 feet each subject, released one per week from March 7th, 1921.

| | |
|---|---|
| Bridlington | Edinburgh |
| Chester | Exeter |
| Riverside London | Torquay |
| Harrogate | The Cornish Riviera |
| Bedford | Loch Lomond |
| Hyde Park | Criccieth |
| Abbeys of Yorkshire | Shrewsbury |
| West End of London | Offas Dyke and Ancient Wales |
| Bempton Cliff Climbers | Hereford |
| Dartmoor | The Lake District |

| | | |
|---|---|---|
| June 16 | | Presentation of Colours by Lord Lieutenant (Lord Nunburnholme), scenes of the ceremony and views of the crowds. |
| August 24 | (S) | R38 Airship Disaster — film of wreckage on the River Humber. |

# List of Films continued

| | |
|---|---|
| August | Film of the Funeral of the Americans killed in the R38 Airship disaster. |
| September | Film of Hull's Industries and Docks at work — sent to Australia, New Zealand, South Africa, and Canada. Sponsored by N.E.H. & B.R. Co. |

## 1922
Gems of the Picturesque North series made in conjuction with the North Eastern Railway Co.

| | |
|---|---|
| Harrogate and Scarborough | 950 ft approx. |
| Knaresborough | 800 ft approx. |
| Whitby | 900 ft approx. |
| York and Bridlington | 900 ft approx. |
| Swaledale | 850 ft approx. |
| Teesdale | 700 ft approx. |
| Runswick Bay and Robin Hood's Bay | 500 ft approx. |
| Filey and Kirkham Abbey | 850 ft approx. |
| Pickering and Whitby by Rail | 900 ft approx. |

## 1923
| | |
|---|---|
| April 14 | War Memorial Dedication Ceremony |
| November 4 | Funeral procession of Peter Jones (famous jockey) |

## 1924
No record of films made.

## 1925
| | | |
|---|---|---|
| August | (S) | Darlington Railway centenary |

## 1926
| | |
|---|---|
| Oct/Nov | Official film of the visit of H.R.H. The Prince of Wales to Hull ('filmed by Mr. E. F. Symmons of Debenham & Co. assisted by Mr. Whitfield of The Tower, Hull'). The film included shots of some Beverlonians and the Mayor, Councillor Wood. |

## 1927
| | | |
|---|---|---|
| May | | Beverley Races (with some excellent shots of the Watt memorial plate). |
| June 18 | (S) | League of Nations Pageant |
| July | | The only successful picture taken of the solar eclipse at Giggleswick. (Photography by Ernest Symmons is uncertain). |
| August 1 | | Territorials at Camp on the Westwood |

## 1928
| | |
|---|---|
| August 1 | 'A film of our Territorial Guests' including arrivals at the station, and marching of the troops to camp including ceremonial parades. (light for filming was bad but in spite of this the film was interesting). |

## 1929
| | | |
|---|---|---|
| April 29 | | Opening of Boys' Migration training hostel. |
| | (S) | 800 (Octo) Centenary 1929 parade |
| | | Riverside Melodies (a song film — sound synchronised with discs). |

# List of Films continued

**1930**
August                    Special Film of our Territorial Guests in Camp ( 600 feet long )

**1931**
No record of films made.

**1932**
May                       Film of local ladies' football match.

**1933**
                          The Saga of Hunmanby
                          The Wonderful Catholic Procession
                          Carnival Queen Competition
                          Film of Hesslewood Orphanage

**1934**
March                     Opening of the Tees Bridge at Middlesbrough by H.R.H. The
                          Duchess of York ( not confirmed as an Ernest Symmons film ).
June                      Carnival Queen competition
September                 Wedding of Miss Mollie Thirsk and Mr. John Botterill

**1935**
April 11                  Laying foundation stone at 'Hull's Super Service Station'
May 12                    Sunday School children assembling and leaving the Market
                          Square for the Wesley chapel.
June                      Coronation of Miss Beverley 1935 ( Miss Dulcie Kilvington ).
June 15                   'Ye Olde English Fayre' ( at Molescroft ).
June 20                   The Babies' competition.
August                    A special film of troops going to the Minster;
                          Cricket season ends; Football season starts; Ladies' Golf
                          tournament;
                          Wedding of Miss Joan Whitehead and Mr. F. Johnson
September                 'The Villain in the Wood' — death watch beetle at St. Mary's
                          Church.
November                  Opening of the season Holderness Hunt.
                          Wedding of Mr. Jack Burnett and Miss Betty Wood at the Minster.
November                  Armistice Sunday in Beverley.
                          Scenes at the Polling Station and declaration of the Poll
November                  Hull Infirmary Cup Tie 2nd Round, Beverley Thursday v West
                          Hull.
                          Corporal M. Marriott decorated with M.B.E. at Victoria Barracks.
                          Shots of the Beverley Amateur Operatic Society.
December                  Short shots of the Wedding of Miss Gladys Harris and Mr. George
                          Redhead at St. Jude's, Hull.

**1936**
January 23                Proclamation of the Accession of King Edward VIII at the Market
                          Cross.
January 28                Memorial Service at the Minster.
January                   Scenes of the laying of the foundation stone of the new Beverley
                          Grammer School.

## List of Films continued

| | | |
|---|---|---|
| July | | Beverley Grmmar School Founder's Day Ceremony at the Minster. |
| | | Items of interest from the Beverley Carnival. |
| August | | Aquatic Sports. |
| | | The 1936 Gymkhana. |
| | | The Holderness Hunt Gymkhana. |
| | | The Holderness Hunt Puppy Walk. |
| | | Puppy Judging at Rise Park. |
| October | | You and Your Dog competition. |
| November | | Opening of the new Grammar School by Viscount Halifax, K.G. |
| | | The One-armed cyclist attempting to break the world record and being welcomed in Beverley. |

**1937**

| | | |
|---|---|---|
| March | | (screened week commencing March 6th). |
| | | Film of some of the industries of Beverley which have been visited by his Worship the Mayor (Mr. C. H. Burden). |
| March | | (screened week commencing March 13th). |
| | | Continuation of the tour of Beverley's industries including the Ropery, Armstrong's and a visit of the East Yorkshire Farmers to British Oil and Cake Mills experimental farm. |
| March | | (screened week commencing March 20th). |
| | | Beverley's industries — Brass Works and Waggon works. |
| May 12 | | Schoolchildren celebrating Coronation Day in the Market Place. |
| | | George Formby — popular comedian, obtaining racing information from Mr. Hammett's horses. |
| | | Childrens' coronation tea at Sparkmill terrace. |
| July | | Territorials in camp on the Westwood. |
| | (S) | Beverley through the Ages. |
| October | (S) | Romance of Leather (sound). |

**1938**

| | |
|---|---|
| | Opening of Armstrong Patents' new factory. |
| | Scenes of the Beverley and East Riding laundry. |
| | Wedding of Dora Cherry to Charles Sheppard. |
| | Wedding of Linda Fisher to Alwyn Middleton. |
| | Wedding of Joyce Bloomfield to Stephen Elder. |
| | Wedding of Joyce Stamford to James Dean. |
| | Hesslewood Orphanage Founders' Day at Holy Trinity Church, Hull (35mm sound film). |

**1939**

| | |
|---|---|
| April | Wedding of Hon. Catherine Hotham and Major Rodger Bower at Dalton Holme. |
| | Wedding of Miss Joyce Slatter and Mr. G. Beard at St. Nicholas' Church, Beverley. |
| June 28 | Scenes at Beverley's National Service Rally. |

**1940**

| | |
|---|---|
| May | Wedding of Miss Audrey Jebson and Flying Officer Jack Powell. |
| August 24 | Scenes at the wedding of Miss Mollie France and Captain J. E. Porter at Beverley Minster. |

91

## List of Films continued

| | | |
|---|---|---|
| October | | Three short plays presented by the pupils of the Girl's High School, St. Mary's School and the Grammar School in aid of the Spitfire Fund. |

**1941**

| | | |
|---|---|---|
| June 14 to 21 | (S) | War weapons week — How to deal with incendiary bombs. |
| August 6 | (S) | The private visit of their Majesties King George VI and Queen Elizabeth to Kingston-upon-Hull. |
| August 26 | | Visit of the Princess Royal to Beverley. |
| September 2 | | British Ambassador to USA visits Hull. |
| | | Helping to buy Beverley's Spitfire. |
| November 7 | | Winston Churchill visits Hull. |

**1942**

| | | |
|---|---|---|
| February | (S) | Warship week. |
| March 12 | | Mrs. Churchill accepts Ambulances for Moscow. |
| July | (S) | Founders' Day parade. |
| August | | Opening of Beverley's wartime nursery and Beverley's Citizens' Advice Bureau. |
| September | | Special Display in the Market Place by Girls of the A.T.S. |

**1943**

| | | |
|---|---|---|
| March 14 | | Beverley Home Guard on Parade. |
| April | | Film of troops entering and leaving the Playhouse Cinema. |
| June | (S) | Wings for Victory week. |
| August | | Safety First |
| August | | Salvage Week. |
| September | | H.R.H. The Princess Royal visits Beverley and the Playhouse Cinema. |
| September | (S) | Battle of Britain anniversary. |

**1944**

| | | |
|---|---|---|
| | | 'My Native Westwood' This film is remembered as being made during the war, and shows the Westwood covered with snow, with people on skis and toboggans. One over-enthusiastic tobogganist knocked the camera over but it continued to run. It is also remembered that Ernest stood to the right of the screen and narrated the film. |
| June | | Scenes of WVS Hospital Helps assisting at the Emergency Hospital. |
| | (S) | Collecting Books for the Forces. |
| | (S) | Canadian troops visit Beverley Minster. |
| December | | Last Home Guard Review. |

**1945**

| | | |
|---|---|---|
| May | (S) | [23] Victory in Europe celebrations — Hull Victory Week (3 reels). |
| | (S) | 'The Man With the Notebook'. |

**1946**

| | | |
|---|---|---|
| May | | [23] Hull Victory celebrations. |
| | | [23] These two films may be one and the same. |

# List of Films continued

| | | |
|---|---|---|
| June 8 | (S) | Peace day celebrations. |
| June | (S) | Freedom of the Borough of Beverley to the East Yorkshire Regiment (1200 feet). |
| August 31 | (S) | Hull City's first match at Boothferry Park. Hull City v Lincoln City, 27,000 crowd, Score 0-0. |

**1947**

| | | |
|---|---|---|
| January | (S) | Freedom of the Borough to Councillor and Mrs. Arthur Watts. |
| May | | Freedom of the Borough to Squadron Leader A. V. Duffill D.F.C. and C.S.M. (Mrs.) Purvis A.T.S. |
| June 1 | | Playhouse News: Wedding of Miss M. Watts and Mr. Donald Jackson at St. Mary's Church, Beverley. |

**1948**

(S) 'The Auction'. This was part of a film conceived by Ernest, which was to tell a story revolving around a Chippendale commode or chest of drawers. The film was to commence at the end of the story when the commode/chest was sold by auction after the family which owned it had fallen upon hard times, compelling them to sell all their posessions. After the auction, the story was to 'flashback' to the 18th century and tell the story of the family who first bought the commode/chest and those who inherited it. Unfortunately the project was dropped.

**1949**
No record of films made.

**1950**
No record of films made.

**1951**
No record of films made.

**1952**
No record of films made.

**1953**

| | |
|---|---|
| January | Short local film of Mayor's welcome to the East Yorkshire Regiment on its journey to Malaysia. |
| April to June. | Baby competition films. |
| September | Launch of the 'George Irwin' at Beverley Shipyard. |

**1954**

| | | |
|---|---|---|
| February | (S) | On location with 'The Lease of Life' at Beverley Minster. |

**1955**
No record of films made.

**1956**
No record of films made.

**1957**
No record of films made.

## List of Films continued

Films of unknown or uncertain dates.

|  | The Pneumatic Tyre. |
| c 1911-1913 | Tricky Tricks — magician at work ( eight half-reel subjects ). |
| c 1912-1916 | [24] Sea Breezes ( 1000 ) feet long ). |
|  | [24] The Life Boat. |
| c 1918 | Presentation of colours to the East Yorkshire Regiment in the Market Place, Beverley. |
| c 1919 | Visit to the Wakefield Dye works by King George V and Queen Mary. ( This visit was recorded on film at the instruction of the Wakefield Town Clerk ). |
| c 1920 | Young Yorkshire — cricket match at Headingley. |
| c 1922 | The Uninvited Guest — a film tribute to actor Hayden Coffin made at the Grand Theatre Hall. |
| c 1933 | Timber Blaze in Hull. |
| c 1935 | It's a Great Life — believed to be the first ever Recruiting Film in which the War Office showed positive interest. |

[24] These two films may be one and the same.